Families & Educators Together

Building Great Relationships that Support Young Children

Derry Koralek, Karen Nemeth, & Kelly Ramsey

National Association for the Education of Young Children

Washington, DC

National Association for the
Education of Young Children
1313 L Street NW, Suite 500
Washington, DC 20005-4101
202-232-8777 • 800-424-2460
NAEYC.org

NAEYC Books

Senior Director, Publishing
and Professional Learning
Susan Friedman

Editor in Chief
Kathy Charner

Senior Editor
Holly Bohart

Editor
Rossella Procopio

Senior Creative Design Manager
Henrique J. Siblesz

Senior Creative Design Specialist
Charity Coleman

Creative Design Specialist
Gillian Frank

Publishing Business
Operations Manager
Francine Markowitz

Through its publications
program, the National
Association for the Education
of Young Children (NAEYC)
provides a forum for discussion
of major issues and ideas in the
early childhood field, with the
hope of provoking thought and
promoting professional growth.
The views expressed or implied
in this book are not necessarily
those of the Association.

Permissions

NAEYC accepts requests for limited use of our copyrighted material.
For permission to reprint, adapt, translate, or otherwise reuse and
repurpose content from this publication, review our guidelines at
NAEYC.org/resources/permissions.

Purchasers of *Families and Educators Together: Building Great
Relationships that Support Young Children* are permitted to photocopy
the content on page 39, 74, and 79 for educational or training purposes
only. Photocopies may be made only from an original book.

Photo Credits

Copyright © Maria Cabrera: 57 (both)

Copyright © Ellen Saint Clair: 8

Copyright © Jenny Levinson: 30 (both)

Copyright © Getty Images: cover photo illustrations,
22, 46, 61, 63, 87, 89, and 102

Library of Congress Control Number: 2018911334

ISBN: 978-1-938113-45-1

Item 1139

Contents

96 Six

Partnering with the Community

Introduction

When you work with young children, you work with their families as well. You partner with families to get to know children and support their development and learning. Families and teachers both have information that can be exchanged as part of an ongoing reciprocal relationship. Together, you support the healthy development and learning of each child.

Families benefit from these partnerships while learning more about child development in general and as applicable to their own children. Research shows that family engagement can enhance children's learning. Researchers at Pennsylvania State University found the following benefits:

> Family engagement in the preschool years contributes to the success of children.

> Children in families with low incomes experience added benefits from their early childhood education when their families are engaged with their child care or school.

> Families with many stress factors including low incomes face more barriers to participating in the school community, though they need the support most, and programs that are most effective respond to the individual needs of diverse families.

> Intensive efforts such as home visiting and parent group membership have the strongest impact on child outcomes. (Bierman, Morris, & Abenavoli 2017)

Family engagement includes the systems and practices used by programs and teachers to enhance connections between families and the early childhood community. It is an essential part of high-quality early childhood education.

Family engagement takes many forms, and you can use a variety of strategies to build meaningful relationships with families. Consider these examples of effective practice.

> Ms. Kerrigan, a family child care provider, knows that once a child turns 2 years old, many families are eager for him to be out of diapers and using the toilet with regularity and ease. She has helped many toddlers learn to use the toilet but wants to acknowledge that each family knows their child best. She shares general information about the readiness signs for this milestone with a resource she found by searching "potty training" on the Zero to Three website (www.zerotothree.org). She encourages families to let her know when they see signs that their child is ready, and when that happens, she partners with the child's family to coordinate a toilet learning approach that works for the family child care program and in the child's home. Their ongoing communication helps to keep family expectations realistic and helps the child achieve this developmental goal.

> The pre-K program at Primrose Lane Elementary School begins in September and ends in June, as do the K–3 classes. At the start of the year, the whole school community is invited to a celebration and orientation picnic. For children who do not have older siblings at the school, this event can be overwhelming. The pre-K teachers plan a series of smaller afternoon get-togethers in the classroom. This allows children and families to feel relaxed while becoming familiar with the setting, teachers, and classmates.

> Every Sunday evening, the families of children in Mr. Schultz's prekindergarten class eagerly await his weekly email newsletter, delivered in Spanish and English. Mr. Schultz recounts the events and experiences of the last week with a focus on what the children are gaining from their activities and how much he enjoys being their teacher. Although family members are encouraged to visit the classroom at any time, he knows that for many working parents, this is quite difficult. His weekly updates give everyone an opportunity to "see" their children's learning.

In these examples, teachers responded to the individual needs and interests of children and families and used a strategy that was a good fit for their setting's distinct features.

Research Says . . .

In the early childhood years, family involvement is clearly related to children's learning outcomes. High levels of family involvement were associated with positive outcomes for children learning literacy, language, math, and social skills in children attending Head Start (Bulotsky-Shearer et al. 2012).

This book offers examples of effective family engagement practices that contribute to mutually respectful and reciprocal relationships that benefit everyone involved. Young children achieve goals jointly set by teachers and family members, teachers witness the outcomes of their intentional efforts, and families gain a sense of confidence as their child's first and forever teachers.

In this book, the focus is on partnerships—the reciprocal process of getting to know individual family members and sharing your own unique characteristics and experiences with them. Each partner learns about the other—interests, cultures, languages, preferred interaction style, assets, abilities, and challenges. Partnerships like this result in meaningful and productive experiences for all.

Family engagement is a big task, and striving to create and implement practices that reflect the diversity of families can seem overwhelming. However, you can use the information in this book to make small changes (e.g., translating and redesigning the infant room sign-in sheet so it is easier for all families to use) or large ones (e.g., creating a family advisory group to provide input and feedback on program practices and policies). The advisory group can help you establish a cohesive approach to engaging families or add to what you already do.

In this book you will find guidance and examples for educators who work directly with children and families, although all early childhood professionals can learn how to support family engagement. Throughout the book, *educator* and *teacher* are used interchangeably to refer to all educators whose days are spent nurturing young children's learning and development in a variety of settings, including family child care homes and classrooms.

The book includes six chapters and an appendix:

> **Chapter 1, "Understanding Family Engagement,"** describes the characteristics of families with young children and summarizes the support for family engagement that comes from local, state, and federal entities.

> **Chapter 2, "The Role of Teachers in a Comprehensive Family Engagement Approach,"** reviews what early childhood programs do to begin developing meaningful reciprocal partnerships with families.

> **Chapter 3, "Family Engagement in Action,"** describes strategies, actions, activities, and projects to make family engagement successful, fun, and rewarding.

> **Chapter 4, "Communicating with Families,"** describes how a program and school can develop a family communication plan that keeps families informed and involved and invites them to partner with educators to support children's development and learning.

> **Chapter 5, "Connecting Home and Program Teaching and Learning,"** defines home–program connections and offers strategies that acknowledge every family's role as their child's prime educator.

> **Chapter 6, "Partnering with the Community,"** reviews the benefits of teaming up with community groups and provides a process for establishing and maintaining partnerships.

> The **Appendix, "Family Engagement Resources,"** is an annotated list of articles, books, and other tools you can use to engage families.

As you finish each chapter, consider the Reflection Questions that appear on the last page. Use them to think about how the content applies to you as a professional and as a member of your early childhood community. These questions can are also useful starting points for study groups that are reading the book and for ongoing staff meetings, coaching, and other forms of professional development about partnering with families.

Understanding Family Engagement

Caring for and teaching someone else's children is a demanding job with enormous expectations. You keep children safe and healthy, nurture their development, and make sure they are challenged enough to learn, but not challenged so much that they can't enjoy feelings of success. You foster and witness key milestones—first steps, first words, and first attempts to write letters and words. And you do all this as part of a team—with colleagues, administrators, specialists, and of course, with children's families. Families are your partners, and the benefits of that partnership remain long after they leave your class or program. This process of reaching out to families, forming reciprocal partnerships, and valuing their contributions to the program is called *family engagement*.

What is family engagement? It's the practice of collaborating with and relating to the family of each child. Some use the term *partnership* to describe relationships with family members. This is another way to emphasize that early educators engage with families because each brings strengths to the relationship that contribute to supporting the child's learning and development. Building these relationships is most important from infancy through the preschool years (Halgunseth et al. 2009).

Family engagement happens when "there is an ongoing, reciprocal, strengths-based partnership between families and their children's early childhood program" (Halgunseth et al. 2009, 3). It includes the overall beliefs, approaches, and strategies used by early childhood educators to form ongoing, mutually beneficial, and meaningful reciprocal relationships with families. As a result, both educators and families encourage children's learning and development. In addition, family members grow as nurturers, mentors, and guides for their children and as individuals whose valuable skills, ideas, and contributions assist their children and their community.

The topics addressed in this chapter include six principles of family engagement, an overview of the characteristics of families with young children, and how governmental and other agencies focus on family engagement.

Learn the Six Principles of Family Engagement

The words in bold are key indicators of successful family engagement. An example follows each principle.

1. Programs invite families to participate in **decision making and goal setting** for their child.

   A teacher might say to a parent: *"Piper seems to have lost interest in dump trucks. Remember last week when we chatted about how playing with the tools and materials at the sand table builds her fine motor skills? What does she like to do at home? I bet we can figure out how you can use similar experiences to support her fine motor skills."*

2. Teachers and programs engage families in **two-way communication**.

   Teachers and families show genuine interest in each other's interests, contributions, and well-being. A teacher might say, *"I know you have concerns about Zoe's vocabulary. Which night this week is best for you to talk with me about it?"* Or, a parent might say, *"Tomas says there's a new pet lizard in the classroom! If you need a family to care for it over the holiday break, we'd love to do it."*

   Teachers invite families to share their family's traditions and customs with the group. In the September newsletter, a provider might note, *"The children love to learn about math and science while cooking. Please share some favorite recipes so we can have the ingredients on hand."*

3. Programs and teachers engage families in ways that are **truly reciprocal**.

   Teachers listen to information provided by families and act on the information to incorporate relevant ideas in the classroom. A parent might tell the teacher, *"I'm starting a new job next month and will be travelling more often. Luciana might have trouble adjusting. I hope we can work together to help her if she needs it."*

   And the teacher could respond, *"Thanks so much for telling me. We have a lot of experience with this. We'll add suitcases and other travel props to the dramatic play area, read books about moms and dads going away for work, and just be available if she needs to talk about her feelings."*

What Is Family Engagement?

Family engagement refers to the systematic inclusion of families in activities and programs that promote children's development, learning, and wellness, including in planning, development, and evaluation. For family engagement to be integrated throughout early childhood systems and programs, providers and schools must engage families as essential partners while providing services that encourage children's learning and development, nurture positive relationships between families and staff, and support families.

(US Department of Health and Human Services, Administration for Children and Families, Children's Bureau, n.d.)

4. Programs provide learning activities for the **home** and in the **community**.

   On the secure classroom website, a teacher posts photos of new take-home backpacks with information about how to foster and build on children's interest in science. The website includes information on how to borrow the backpacks.

   A parent shares her excitement and offers to contribute materials for new backpacks when the children are no longer interested in the ones that are currently available.

5. Programs invite families to participate in **program-level decisions and wider advocacy efforts.**

   A program receives funding from a local business to revamp the playground and update it with safe surfaces. The program shares this good news and schedules a meeting to discuss ways to enhance the playground. At the meeting, families review and provide input on what materials and equipment provide the greatest level of safety, open-ended play, and skill development.

6. Programs implement a comprehensive **program-level system.**

   The program-wide newsletter features updates on each classroom's family engagement experiences.

   A colorful banner at the door to the program features the word *Welcome* in multiple languages along with a collection of images of children that reflect the families in the program (NAEYC, n.d.).

There are many layers to the important work of building relationships with all families. When these six principles of family engagement are implemented, educators and families work together to ensure high-quality education for children.

There is no one-size-fits-all approach to family engagement. Just as an early childhood curriculum is individualized to respond to each child's unique characteristics, effective programs establish and tailor a variety of family engagement strategies to match the interests, assets, culture, composition, and home languages of individual families. One child's family members may be eager to spend time in the classroom and have a schedule that permits them to do so regularly. For another child, whose parents are at work during the day, classroom visits are rarely possible; they stay engaged through daily conversations, texts, or email exchanges. Tailor the family engagement approaches and specific strategies you use to reflect the characteristics of the community and individual children and families. For example, a teacher at an employer-supported toddler child care program in Los Angeles sends an email with pictures and a daily summary to families before pick-up time. Busy families are happy to use this information on the ride home to chat with their child about his day, to sing songs, or to repeat stories the teacher described. Throughout this book, look for additional examples of effective practices like this one.

Define What a Family Is

In this book, *family* is defined as one or more children and the adults who have sole or shared primary responsibility for the children's well-being as the child's guardian and primary caregivers. A family can include adults who are the child's biological or adoptive parents, other close family members, or other individuals such as foster families and guardians who are committed to supporting the child emotionally, financially, or both. Family members may live in

Identifying and Addressing the Needs of New Residents

Jamie Hartley is the director of the Methodist Day School (MDS) in Portland, TX, which is a ministry of First United Methodist Church of Portland. The school was formed by the Education Committee of the church in 1990 to meet the needs of families and young children in the community. It operates during the school calendar year and serves children who are 18 months to 4 years old.

CHALLENGE
After an increase in industrial jobs in our area, many young families moved to our community in a short period of time. The families were unfamiliar with the area and isolated while their partners worked long hours. We wanted to step in to help families get to know each other so they could build friendships in their new locale. Family members also had questions about their children, including how to handle challenging behaviors and general questions about child development. Finding a way to meet both needs was important to us.

STRATEGY
Dana, a member of First United Methodist Church was instrumental in developing this group. She came up with the name (e)Mpower and designed it to be a group of 10 to 12 family members who gather each week to share the joys and challenges of parenting. In the second year of operation, a parent offered to be the regular facilitator, and group members take turns providing snacks. The family members, mostly mothers, appreciate being able to gather in a comfortable environment to establish friendships, exchange ideas, and discuss parenting challenges.

RESULTS
An unanticipated outcome was that the group members volunteered to organize school events such as Western Days, a two-day event through which children learn about Texas Independence Day. A parent committee plans the event which includes art, music, cooking, and outdoor activities focused on the state's history. This committee also organizes the MDS booth at the community Book-a-Palooza to promote reading for young children.

UPDATE
Our school now uses a curriculum as the foundation for the meetings and suggests resources for families to review on their own.

Since many of the family members have younger children, we now include the cost for child care and snacks in the school's annual budget, making it easier for family members to attend the meetings. In addition, we reserve the meeting space a year in advance to make sure there is always space for our group to meet. We now have anywhere from 15–17 parents attending each week, as well as three parent facilitators for (e)Mpower. Year after year, it continues to grow, developing lasting friendships, offering support and encouragement, and empowering families to be their best.

the same household or in different households. Families have one or more children living with a wider range of adult nurturers, including but not limited to

> Two married parents

> Two unmarried parents

> A single adult—mother, father, or other family member such as a grandparent

> Grandparents or other adult family members

> Blended families formed when parents remarry and combine households

> Foster and group-home families formed when a child's parents and relatives are not able to care for him or her

Throughout this book, the terms *parent* and *family* are used interchangeably.

Replace Parent Involvement with Family Engagement

Early childhood educators sometimes use the term *parent involvement* to describe conscious efforts to inform families and encourage their participation in their child's learning. Merely *involving* families in their child's education, however, can have the unintended consequence of making parents feel like helpers who follow the teacher's directions rather than equal partners.

True family engagement, on the other hand, involves teachers building a relationship with families, learning how families are interested in being involved in their child's learning, and working with families to determine how they want to be engaged and their preferred times and methods for exchanging information about their child's experiences. Family engagement includes a wide range of approaches and activities—some that take place at home and others in the community or the classroom or program. For example, if a family's home language is one that other children in your class speak, and this family is interested in supporting other families who speak that language, you might ask a member of this family to create home-language versions of the volunteer sign-up forms that you use during enrollment home visits—a task she can do at home because she works during the day. Another parent, a nurse who works an evening shift and is interested in children's early literacy, might visit the program during the day to read to individual children.

Parental involvement typically refers to parents' participation in the systems and activities that promote a child's well-being. The term *family engagement* implies that this responsibility falls on more than just the parents: siblings, relatives, and even friends play an important role (Weyer 2015). It relies on ongoing reciprocal engagement and communication with all family members.

Build Strong Relationships Between Families and Educators

Family engagement is founded on strong relationships between all who play a role in children's care and education. Family members and educators develop, maintain, and enhance their relationships with each other. As an early childhood educator, you get to know family members and allow families to get to know you, as all of you share the personal experiences, assets, and interests that you bring to the classroom. Your work to engage families will develop reciprocal relationships, involving equal partners.

Reciprocity also applies to the information about individual children shared by each of the partners. You ask for and use the information families provide to enhance the program for individual children and for the group. For example, a father might share a short cell phone video showing 26-month-old Yancey scrambling eggs for breakfast. You respond by placing several whisks in the basket of water play props to encourage Yancey and other children to practice using this tool. Families value and apply the information you provide. When you tell Iris's mom that Iris thoroughly enjoyed collecting leaves on the class nature walk, her mom plans a Saturday outing to the park. Both families and educators contribute valuable input to enhance a child's learning and development.

Another element of the partnership between educators and family members is that each partner contributes specific expertise. Families are the experts about their child. They know how he interacts with members of the family and with strangers; how he responds to new foods and new situations; what he likes to play with; and how he shows what his needs and interests are. On the other hand, you can share and build on similar information that you learned from observing him and apply your knowledge of child development and best practices to foster his development.

SmartStart: Reaching Out to the Waiting List

Renate Engels is the director of the Guadalupe Center's Early Childhood Education Center in Immokalee, FL, which serves more than 300 children from infancy through age 5. More than 40 percent of Immokalee's families have incomes below the federal poverty level, and almost every public school student qualifies for free lunches.

CHALLENGE
: The waiting list for attendance at the Guadalupe Center reached 500 children. We recognized an unmet need—there were not enough spaces in quality early childhood programs to serve the families who live in our community. This lack of full access to early childhood programs contributes to more than 80 percent of kindergartners in Immokalee arriving at school without the skills needed to succeed. To address this situation we created an early learning program for children and families on the center's waiting list.

STRATEGY
: We developed a new program, SmartStart, which is offered once a week in centrally located sites. Our goal is to build rapport with families who face barriers to accessing preschool providers. Through SmartStart, children learn and play with peers. Parents gain the knowledge they need to help their children learn the skills they need to be successful in kindergarten, including social and emotional skills. As needed, the Guadalupe Center connects families with outside social service organizations.

RESULTS
: The weekly SmartStart classes focused on all areas of development. By the end of the school year, 82 percent of the children met or exceeded expectations, especially in cognitive areas. In addition, we used tablets and the Duolingo app to help parents who are learning to speak English. Weekly activity packages to use at home included a book, a drawing activity, and a craft exploration.

UPDATE
: The Guadalupe Center has expanded the program to include families who are not on the center's waiting list. We have partnered with libraries, schools, and other groups within the community to make it easier for families to get to SmartStart. Seventy-five children in SmartStart meet at five separate locations Monday through Friday.

Get to Know Your Community

You can add to what you know and understand about the families of the children in your class by getting to know more about the community around your school or program. Each community has traditions and beliefs that tie residents together, and each family has characteristics that make them unique. Even if all families use the same home language or come from the same culture, it's likely that each individual family has a distinct structure, home life, and goals for their children. If you're not familiar with the local community and where families spend time, walk or ride through the local neighborhoods and visit shops, restaurants, and parks. Some teachers attend local events such as religious services or cultural festivals to connect with the lives of the children and their families. The more you know and understand about the environment and everyday experiences of the children and families, the easier it will be to build genuine connections with families and work together to support their children. Getting to know families is an ongoing process that begins even before a child enters the program. Initial and ongoing communication strategies are discussed in Chapter 4, "Communicating with Families."

Learn About Families

All families have their own unique cultural context. In some families, everyone has the same or a similar background. Families may also be diverse, with individuals who speak two or more languages, identify as members of different races, were born in the United States or in another country, or many other characteristics.

Another aspect is the age of the adult family members. Teen parents are likely to have different interests and characteristics than grandparents who are the child's primary caregiver. Forty percent of the millennial generation are parents. Gross and O'Neil-Hart (2017), who studied families in which one parent was the child's father and the other was the child's mother, found that millennial parents share certain beliefs and approaches to parenting, including the following:.

> One-third follow traditional gender roles.

> One-third share chores equally.

> One-third want to share equally but find that, actually, the female parent handles more of the caregiving and child-rearing responsibilities.

> Forty-five percent of millennial moms stay home to raise their children.

> They tend to accept their children's non-gender-conforming choices in clothing, toys, experiences, and so on.

> Many millennial fathers see involvement with children as a positive masculine trait.

> Three-fourths value a good work/life balance.

> They tend to know a lot about child development but may suffer from information overload because information is readily available via the internet and social media.

> They are safety conscious and search for and use information on keeping their children safe.

> They are more likely than older parents to say parents could never be too involved in their children's education; overall, 61 percent of millennial parents say parents can never be too involved, compared with 52 percent of Gen X parents and 51 percent of Baby Boomer parents.

To learn more about the characteristics of young families, ages 18 to 24, read *Opening Doors for Young Parents,* a policy report from the Annie E. Casey Foundation (2018). The authors provide research, data, and examples of successful approaches to supporting children and their parents.

Virtual and In-Person Strategies (VIPs): Acknowledging Preferences of New Generations

Melissa Russell is preschool director at The Hundred Acre School at Heritage Museums and Gardens in Sandwich, MA. Founded in 2014, the school is a full-day prekindergarten program for approximately 40 children and seven teachers in three STEM-focused classrooms. The museums and 100-acre gardens are an extension of the classroom-based activities and experiences.

CHALLENGE

When we opened the school, we knew family engagement should and would be a key part of our program. The families are either millennials or at the end of Generation X. The Gen X families use digital media but also like to exchange information through written and verbal exchanges. Most millennial families prefer to use digital methods. Our strategies must fit families' preferences.

STRATEGY

We decided to include families physically and virtually in our daily experiences as active partners in extending the curriculum. Thus, Virtual and In-Person Strategies (VIPs) was born. The VIPs experience focuses on environment, communication, education, and partnerships.

1. Our **environment** is inviting and supportive. Smiling teachers welcome all and communicate that all are valued members of the community.

2. **Communications** are in print, posted in the building and sent home; in positive person-to-person interactions; and through individualized texts and an app that supports sharing of photos, videos, notes, PDFs, and URLs.

3. We believe **education** is for everyone, including families. Children and teachers summarize each day on a "think time board" and display it on an easel during pick-up times. We also post a photo of the board in our online app for family members who were not at pick-up time. Families can use information on the boards as conversation starters and ask questions to extend children's learning.

4. We celebrate families through **partnerships** and classroom experiences. Through classroom visits, called Profession Spotlight, families can share their expertise with the children.

RESULTS

I realized our family engagement was effective when families began telling us about the ways they extend the curriculum at home. They are grateful for the ways in which they can feel a part of their child's daily experiences. The app is effective because it allows for "instant" exchanges of information.

UPDATE

We continue to use our VIPs method with tremendous success and high levels of family engagement. Recently, almost 250 family and community members came to our year-end celebration, further proving the value of connecting ideas and people.

Data about young children, families, and specific populations in the United States are interesting, informative, and available online in reports from the US Census and other groups. Numbers help you notice trends and changes so you can adapt your practices to fit children and families. In your daily work, however, the numbers are never as important as that one unique child in front of you or that individual family you are getting to know.

Over time, you will be able to see the value and results of your family engagement efforts. Relationships with families will be more meaningful, and children will thrive because the most important people in their lives are working together. An important part of the relationship-building process is to identify and build on the strengths of individuals. Focusing on parents' skills and interests, rather than defining their needs, shows respect and serves to forge reciprocal relationships, in which each partner is appreciated and valued for their contributions to supporting the child.

Five Things Teachers Should Know About Parents

Zero to Three, in partnership with the Bezos Family Foundation, published the National Parent Survey Report, *Tuning In: Parents of Young Children Tell Us What They Think, Know, and Need* (2016). Researchers held in-home discussions and conducted a national survey of a diverse group of millennial and Generation X parents. Their findings included the following conclusions:

1. Parents are proud of raising their children, but they also recognize the challenges that come with the job. Ninety percent of parents said parenting is their greatest joy, but 70 percent said it was also their biggest challenge. Teachers can help families define and address these challenges.

2. Parents need and want information and support. Eighty percent of parents work to be better parents, and the majority say if they knew more parenting strategies, they would use them. However, almost half of parents say they aren't getting what they need to cope with times of stress. Teachers can help by forming trusting partnerships with parents and connecting them with useful resources.

3. It is important to make connections with uncles, grandfathers, and male family caregivers, who are more motivated than ever and want to be involved in their child's life and education. As an example, in this study about half of the dads said they didn't know where to find information they could trust. Teachers can suggest ways to get the entire family involved.

4. Parents have a difficult time finding resources they trust. Six in 10 parents are skeptical of advice that comes from people who do not know their child and his or her situation. Teachers can connect parents with research-based resources, such as those on NAEYC's For Families site (NAEYC.org/our-work/for-families), that fit their specific needs. Most parents like websites or blogs created by experts.

5. What do parents want to know? They want current research on children's emotional and brain development. They also want to learn about self-control and developmental milestones so they will know what is age-appropriate. Moreover, they want information on effective discipline and strategies to help them be more patient, which many parents see as the biggest challenge of being a parent.

Adapted from D. Riser, "5 Things Teachers Should Know About Parents" (March 2018): NAEYC.org/resources/blog/5-things-teachers-should-know-about-parents. The full report is available on the Zero to Three website: www.zerotothree.org.

Learn About the Sources of Support for Family Engagement

There are many policies, websites, resources, and experts available to inform your work with families. These include local, state, and federal policies and guidance; requirements for program accreditation; and standards for professional development. In addition, as described in Chapter 3 of this book, each program can develop family engagement practices that reflect the children and families in their early childhood setting, the responsibilities outlined in job descriptions, the program's supervision and coaching priorities, and the local community.

In some early childhood settings, family engagement practices are already in place, often to meet requirements set by funders or licensing agencies. In others, teachers, principals, directors, and other leaders have made family engagement a priority and included it in program and individual performance assessments. Here are a few examples of the kinds of support that ensure the success of family engagement efforts.

Head Start

Head Start's long history of services focused on both children and their families is a key part of the program design. Since implementation of its first programs in the summer of 1965, Head Start has acknowledged the important role of families through policies, regulations, and practices. The phrase "Parents are children's first teachers" exemplifies the Head Start commitment to engaging families in their children's care and education. Whether your program is or is not a Head Start program, the Head Start Program Performance Standards US Office of Head Start (2016) offer useful guidance on family engagement priorities.

Head Start's Early Childhood Learning and Knowledge Center (ECLKC) is a digital library of print, audio, and video resources that can be used in all early childhood settings. See the Family Engagement page of the ECLKC website for family engagement tools you might find useful: https://eclkc.ohs.acf.hhs.gov/family-engagement.

US Department of Education

At the federal government level, the US Department of Education provides monthly newsletters, toolkits, and other resources on family engagement: www.ed.gov/parent-and-family-engagement

In 2018, the department's Office of Innovation and Improvement, Statewide Family Engagement Centers Program, awarded 11 grants in 11 states to organizations to establish statewide family engagement centers. Each center will offer comprehensive training and technical assistance to support home–school partnerships.

State Education Agencies

Most state education agency staff would agree that family engagement is an important practice in early childhood settings. Several states have gone further, however, by implementing innovative approaches. The National Association for Family, School, and Community Engagement (NAFSCE) highlights state successes in engaging families on its State Policy page: https://nafsce.site-ym.com/page/StatePolicy. Descriptions of a few of the state approaches are included in the Appendix on page 126.

Family Engagement Fosters Success for Children with Disabilities

Valerie Rocio Harvey is a national board certified teacher at the Expanded Transitional Kindergarten/Preschool Collaborative Class at Lankershim Elementary in North Hollywood, CA. The class is a general education setting, and it includes children who have been identified as developmentally delayed, have an IEP plan, and receive designated instructional services. It is considered a full inclusion model where the children with IEPs are learning alongside their peers.

CHALLENGE

The preschoolers I teach have stronger skills in the use of digital tools than in social, language, and literacy development. Some have a limited interest in the world around them. Families want to help support their children's development through fun home activities that build on classroom learning.

STRATEGY

For each new study unit, I invite families to visit and hear about what the children will be learning. I introduce key terms and encourage families to engage their children in science at home and in the community. For example, for our trees study, families and children could go to the park to investigate how leaves from one tree are different from another. When we do bark or leaf rubbings, some families join our trip to the park. I model helping children use language and their senses to describe what they see, how leaves feel, how rough bark feels against skin, and so on. Families can use similar practices to extend learning at home. For family members who can't visit the classroom, I ask for permission to record and share children's explorations on my cellphone so the families can listen to these recordings at home.

RESULTS

Family engagement increased, including the families of two children who have IEPs with an eligibility of speech and language impairment. Initially, the children had difficulty in communicating, and both struggled to make themselves understood. Both families came to class and watched me work with their children. They asked for duplicate materials so they could use them at home. The parents loved receiving videos of their children. With all of us working together, the children made significant progress. Their success was a testament to their families' engagement.

UPDATE

I continue to engage families and encourage them to take advantage of natural teachable moments. I want the children to see, feel, and hear the wonders of the world around them and not rely only on digital tools.

Many states have also adopted all or portions of the National Standards for Family–School Partnerships developed by the National PTA: www.pta.org/home/run-your-pta/National -Standards-for-Family-School-Partnerships

State Quality Rating and Improvement Systems (QRIS)

Most states, the District of Columbia, and the US territories have or are in the process of implementing quality rating and improvement systems (QRIS) to assess and improve the quality of early childhood and school-age care and education programs. Parent and family involvement is one indicator of quality included by 90 percent of the states with active QRIS (2016). Child Care Aware of America, a national association for child care resource and referral agencies, completed a literature review of quality family engagement practices that can be measured through QRIS. These are organized in four feature categories: "communication, utilizing family needs and feedback to inform the program, collaborative activities with families, and providing community resource referrals and family support" (Child Care Aware of America, n.d., 3).

> Communication: Educators and families use varied and flexible methods that encourage information exchanges in the family's home language. Communication builds respectful relationships between educators and families.

> Using family needs and feedback: Educators learn about the needs and goals of the children and families they serve by conducting surveys, inviting comments, holding exit interviews, and reviewing assessments of strengths and needs. Using this information helps programs connect with families in creative and meaningful ways.

> Collaboration with families: Educators provide many meaningful opportunities for families to take part in a child's early care and education. Successful activities ensure families are equal partners in promoting healthy child development and skills.

> Community resources and family support: Educators advocate for services and resources for which families express a need. They link families with community resources and offer parenting and family education support.

QRIS is widely used to provide information for families and for anyone concerned with the quality of early childhood programs. Reviewing and rating family engagement efforts is a key way to ensure early childhood programs are developing meaningful partnerships with families.

Support from Your State

To find out how your state attends to family engagement in care and education settings, visit the US Department of Education's website and look for your state: www2.ed.gov/about/contacts/state/index.html.

You can also visit the website of the National Association of Early Childhood Specialists in State Departments of Education (NAECS-SDE): www.naecs-sde.org. NAECS-SDE members include state education agency staff members with major responsibilities in the field of early childhood education, from infancy through the early elementary grades.

Keep Literacy Learning in Focus All Summer Long

Tracy Ehlert is the owner of B2K Learning Center in Cedar Rapids, Iowa, which is licensed to serve 12 children from birth through school age. The program offers a safe, loving, stimulating, developmentally appropriate, anti-bias, and play-based environment.

CHALLENGE

In the summer, our program has more field trips and special activities than at other times of the year. We still read daily, but we noticed that some children forget the literacy learning that took place during the year. Families also say they find they aren't reading as much to their children in the summer, due to their children's busy schedules. I decided to plan a fun child-led literacy project that would engage families while children planned and made decisions about using the materials.

STRATEGY

We surveyed families to determine their interest in this idea, then looked for materials to fit (a) our budget, (b) the children's ages, (c) learning objectives, and (d) ease of use by children and adults with varied skill levels. We created Summer Literacy Boxes that families could borrow for a week at a time during the summer months. Each box had books related to a theme and quick, fun activities that promote literacy, as well as other areas like math, fine motor skills, large motor skills, and art. A parent handout on literacy was included to encourage daily reading and suggest ways to promote learning at home. The boxes contained everything needed to complete activities—down to the crayons and glue—to ensure that all families could complete every activity. The boxes were small and easy to transport, and the activities could be done almost anywhere (in the car, while waiting for appointments, while dinner is being prepared, etc.).

RESULTS

The project had 100 percent participation—a rare occurrence for our projects. We fulfilled some family engagement goals and promoted children's literacy skills. The families stayed engaged all summer, and the children were excited about reading and the activities they did with their families. Children's literacy skills were maintained or enhanced.

UPDATE

We continue to survey family needs and their interests. They are still eager to use the Summer Literacy Boxes, and we are adding a new set of boxes for next summer.

Learn About Standards and Requirements for Family Engagement

National organizations, including NAEYC and the Council for Professional Recognition, have addressed family engagement in their requirements and resources.

NAEYC

NAEYC's position statements are grounded in NAEYC's core values, emphasizing diversity and inclusion, research-based teaching, and knowledge of child development. The following statements underscore the complex and critical ways in which early childhood educators promote early learning through their relationships—with children, families, and colleagues—that are embedded in a broader societal context.

Establishing reciprocal relationships with families and respecting families' cultural assets are core to developmentally appropriate practice (DAP). "Developmentally appropriate practices derive from deep knowledge of child development principles and of the program's children in particular, as well as the context within which each of them is living. The younger the child, the more necessary it is for practitioners to acquire this particular knowledge through relationships with children's families" (NAEYC 2009, 22).

Family partnerships are part of Standard 2 of NAEYC's forthcoming position statement on professional standards and competencies for early childhood educators: An important aspect of being a competent and knowledgeable early childhood professional includes developing partnerships with children's families, including knowing, understanding, and valuing the importance of and diversity in families and in the community. Teachers use this understanding to develop respectful, culturally and linguistically responsive, reciprocal relationships with families.

NAEYC's forthcoming position statement on equity guides educators to think about equity and diversity as they work with families:

> Embrace the primary role of families in children's development and learning.

> Recognize and acknowledge family members based on the composition the family defines.

> Seek to learn about and honor each family's childrearing values, language (including dialects), and culture.

> As much as possible, uphold families' right to make decisions for and with their children. If a family's desire conflicts with your professional knowledge, seek to identify common goals and mutually acceptable strategies.

Standard 7 of NAEYC's Early Learning Program Standards addresses relationships with families. "The program establishes and maintains collaborative relationships with each child's family to foster children's development in all settings. These relationships are sensitive to family composition, language, and culture. To support children's optimal learning and development, programs need to establish relationships with families based on mutual trust and respect, involve families in their children's educational growth, and encourage families to fully participate in the program" (NAEYC 2018, 91).

NAEYC also addresses family engagement through a resource-filled website (NAEYC.org/our-work/for-families) devoted to topics of interest to families with young children. The website is also a valuable tool for educators' family engagement efforts.

The Council for Professional Recognition

The Council for Professional Recognition issues the Child Development Associate (CDA) Credential for early childhood educators in home or family child care settings serving children from birth through age 5. The CDA is organized in six Competency Standards and 13 Professional Areas. Professional Area 11, Families, comes under Competency Standard 4, "To establish positive and productive relationships with families." Credentialing requires that the candidate "establishes a positive, responsive, and cooperative relationship with each child's family, engages in two-way communication with families, encourages their involvement in the program, and supports the child's relationship with his or her family" (Washington 2017, 6).

This brief description of how funders, states, and national professional groups support family engagement reinforces the importance of this part of early childhood programs. As noted in *Essentials for Working with Young Children* (Washington 2017), the textbook used by CDA candidates seeking accreditation:

> It is important to remember . . . that parents are a child's first and forever teachers. Early childhood educators contribute to learning during an important stage of a young child's life. But families are forever. In most cases they will care for, nurture, and educate their child throughout childhood. (435)

Throughout this book, you will find practical, easy-to-use ideas and information to enhance your work with children and families, a rewarding part of being an early childhood educator.

Reflection Questions

Now that you have read this chapter, consider the following questions:

1. How does your program implement family engagement practices? How do those practices reflect the research on what teachers should know about families that appear on page 13?

2. In what ways do you think families want to contribute to their child's development and learning? How can you learn about their interests and preferred engagement options?

3. What does your program do to ensure that family engagement is a priority for teachers and other staff? What family engagement support do you get from coaches, supervisors, colleagues, and more?

TWO

The Role of Teachers in a Comprehensive Family Engagement Approach

Children thrive when they have the skills they need to succeed and when their families are meaningfully involved in their development and learning (Bierman, Morris, & Abenavoli 2017).

Although you will engage with families using strategies that work for you and represent your individuality as a teacher, you are not alone in this work. Truly effective family engagement is ensured by the way each teacher functions as part of a program- or school-wide system. Every person who works in a program contributes to effective family engagement, and a successful system makes sure those roles are clearly defined and well-supported. This is the focus of the sixth principle of family engagement:

> Programs implement a comprehensive program-level system of family engagement. Programs institutionalize family engagement policies and practices and ensure that teachers, administrators, and other staff receive the supports they need to fully engage families. (NAEYC, n.d.)

Establishing an effective family engagement system for an early childhood program takes time, full staff involvement, and thoughtful reflection on processes and procedures. You might have seen family engagement mentioned in your job description, included in the program calendar, or addressed in professional development. These are all elements of a cohesive system.

As an example, the Educare early childhood programs across the country approach family engagement with a dual focus: (1) building a relationship with each family and (2) developing a program-wide system that includes and supports all families. Every Educare program emphasizes strong parent–child relationships, school–family partnerships, and parent support for learning (Educare Learning Network 2015).

> "We believe the most profound impact we can have on children and families is to use the vehicle of strong, nurturing relationships," says Portia Kennel, senior advisor of the Buffett Early Childhood Fund and founding executive director of Educare Learning Network. (2015, 1)

Early childhood teachers are most successful in their work with families when they have the following kinds of supports, which are topics discussed in this book.

1. Orientation and professional development to build their family engagement knowledge and skills

2. Resources to create a welcoming environment for families

3. Support for getting to know families, such as home visiting guidance

4. Program-wide supports, such as family engagement written into policies, job descriptions, and family handbooks

5. Specific guidance about enhancing the curriculum with family engagement at the program and at home

6. Opportunities to partner with members of the community in support of family engagement

This chapter describes strategies you can use to get to know each family as they learn about and enter your program. Also included are ways teachers can participate effectively within a program-wide family engagement system. These ideas may help you and your colleagues build or enhance such a system. What kinds of information and support do you need to feel confident about building and sustaining meaningful relationships with families?

Participate in Professional Development

Every staff member—teachers, assistant teachers, administrators, substitute and floating teachers, specialists, coaches, custodians, directors, bus drivers, and more—is a program ambassador and plays a role in building relationships with families. This means that all staff can benefit from professional development experiences that help them learn, reflect on, and understand more about the value of engaging with families of young children—in general, and those whose children attend the program. In addition, professional development can review the benefits of family engagement—for families, children, and staff—and examine participants' beliefs and practices related to building reciprocal partnerships with families. As with other kinds of professional development, learning about family engagement is ongoing and may take various forms. Onsite coaching, watching videos of actual practice, reading articles and books, and participating in learning communities are all useful ways to learn about family engagement. Ask former and current families, who are great sources of information, to help you

To learn about a framework for family relationships, see *Building Partnerships: Guide to Developing Relationships with Families,* which is available on the website of the Office of Head Start's Early Childhood Learning and Knowledge Center. The authors provide research, data, and examples of successful approaches to supporting children and families and recommendations for using a strengths-based approach.

> Identify families' interests, abilities, and assets

> Plan family engagement activities that value families' abilities and assets

> Address the needs of children and families

> Plan family engagement activities in formats that work for the children's families

At the beginning of the year and throughout the year when new staff join the program, some programs assess staff development needs and interests and review the learning formats staff members prefer. In addition to making suggestions for your program's professional development plans, you can create your own professional development plan that addresses family engagement and other topics.

It's important to also address needs as they arise. For example, "A child with spina bifida is joining my class. What do I need to know so I can welcome this child and her family and partner with them?" Other times, you may need information and skills that are related to an interest that is not covered in the annual professional development plan. "We all know how important reading aloud is for young children. I'd like to encourage families to use simple read-aloud tips. One idea is to learn how to make brief videos about the benefits of reading aloud to children."

Contribute to Program-Wide Support for Families

Here are some strategies that programs may use as part of their approach to setting the stage for effective family engagement. The work of each teacher is important individually and in the context of overall program policies and practices. When a program has a family engagement system, teachers can develop and use strategies that fit within the overall goals and priorities of the system. If there is not a system, or it is still under development, teachers can refer to NAEYC's six principles of family engagement for guidance. Typically, teachers participate in designing the family engagement approach and in regularly assessing and updating it to make sure it works for the families whose children are enrolled in the program. The following sections offer some ideas that you can support at your program, along with ways that you can participate in program-wide efforts. They include creating an environment that welcomes families, handling initial inquiries, conducting informational meetings, and taking part in enrollment and transitions.

Create a Welcoming Environment

An environment that welcomes families involves both people and things. All members of an early childhood community are on the "welcoming committee" because each interaction can contribute to the success of every child and family. Anyone could be the first person a family sees when they arrive. Families' often form their first impression of your program or school at the entrance. What message does your entrance communicate to families and visitors? Do the signs, displays, and information reflect the diversity of your community? Some places have large entrances and others have small ones. What matters most is that they send a clear message to all children and families: "We welcome you to our learning community and value your involvement." The following are examples of how two settings, using different approaches, clearly communicate that children and families are welcome and respected.

> At the Learning Together Child Care Center, the entrance is a grand piazza where adults can linger as they drop off their children and talk with other families. The space is filled with comfortable couches, fluffy floor pillows, plants, and whimsical displays featuring pictures of families laughing, playing, and having fun. The cheerful setting says, "Welcome! Come in and stay for a while."

> At Mrs. Pandey's family child care home, there are always two comfortable chairs by the front door where family members feel welcome to sit and have a chat when dropping off or picking up their children. When families stop by, they might see a child playing with friends or notice artwork that Mrs. Pandey has displayed at children's eye level. Children and families feel respected and understood by this family child care provider because the space facilitates conversations and supports relationships.

Warm and inviting entry spaces, such as the ones described above, convey the message that your site welcomes families to the program. At any point a prospective or current family member can talk with a staff member, have their questions answered, and receive suggestions for next steps. With that positive start, many visiting families will go on to enroll their child in your program.

Handle Initial Inquiries and Visits with Care

Partnerships with families begin the moment they inquire about your program—on the phone or in person. Although teachers are usually in their classrooms when families call and therefore don't handle the initial calls or visits, it's important for everyone to know how the program welcomes families. When a parent hears a staff member's welcoming voice, the relationship with the program begins. This interaction sets the tone for how you partner together. Strike a welcoming, friendly tone in this interaction. If it is on the phone, smile while talking, just as you would when you meet and greet families in person.

Here is an example of a great first impression:

The Perez Family's First Impression

When the Perez family—mother, father, and abuela—walk into the Creative Discoveries Early Head Start Program, they hear soft music playing and see an array of photos of children and teachers engaged in learning and family members interacting with staff. The front office staff smile and warmly greet the family members. "Good morning. How can I help you?" The family returns the smile and the relationship begins.

All relationships are established on a sense of trust. Such trust is assumed before there have been enough interactions to truly establish it. When both families and educators maintain that trust, meaningful, reciprocal connections can result from that trust and move the relationship forward.

A key to building trust is giving each person time and space to share information about who they are and to express their needs. The first time families ask about your program is an opportunity to set the tone for working together in partnership.

Plan Engaging Informational Meetings

Part of a family engagement system is determining how best to hold informational meetings with families. These get-togethers are often scheduled after a family lets you know they are interested in your program or school. Follow the steps described below and adapt them as needed.

1. Choose a Location

Hold informational meetings in spaces that are free of distractions. Include a variety of simple open-ended materials for children of different ages to explore while the adults discuss the program's highlights. Speak clearly using short sentences and jargon-free vocabulary. When meeting with families who use languages you do not speak, a quiet location makes it easier for everyone to understand each other. If you do not speak the family's home language, arrange for a translator to assist you. Keep in mind that family members may have a wide range of literacy levels in English, or in other home languages. If a translator is not available, be prepared with a computer or tablet so you can access translation apps or use images and videos to support communication.

For example, a family child care provider welcomes families to visit during the hours of operation. While the children who are enrolled in her program play and look at books, she explains to a visiting family what the children are doing and learning as a way to present the program to the family. When a baby wakes from his nap, she responds to the baby's needs, demonstrating that she is skilled at caring for a multiage group. The visiting family sees and hears how she will interact with and support their child.

Welcome All Families

> Display signs or posters that say "hello" or "welcome" in several languages. These can be posted throughout the building, including in classrooms.

> Include informative signs in languages that the children and their families speak. For example, "Please Sign In Here" or "The Parking Lot Is Behind This Building" or "We Use Google Translate." Teachers can make signs in various languages and illustrate them with photos to identify learning centers and explain what children learn in each center.

> Provide materials, art, and books for children that reflect the cultures and diversity of their community. Use visuals to convey your celebration of all families, including their culture, languages, and ethnicities. Make sure dolls and dramatic play props and dress-up clothes are culturally appropriate.

> When you learn that a family coming to visit your program speaks a language that is not on your posters, add a sign or poster to welcome that family in their home language. Learn a few welcoming words in the language and how to correctly pronounce their names.

2. Arrange the Space to Promote Relaxed Connections

As much as possible, reduce physical barriers that could interfere with getting to know each other in a genuine way. Sit in comfortable chairs next to the family or at a small table, rather than behind a desk with the family members seated across from you. Also, think about the waiting area. Does it welcome connections and conversations or remind families of a doctor's office?

For example, a child development program created a small family reception area with comfortable chairs, a water cooler and cups, side tables with lamps, and a computer screen displaying a looped PowerPoint file with images of children's activities. Whether families were first-time visitors or coming in for a scheduled meeting, they walked into a relaxing, respectful space.

3. Be Prepared

When any family visits, they will have a lot to remember after they return home. Provide a welcome packet about the program with information in the languages of your community and in English. It can include

> A few brief handouts that share basic information about the program's philosophy, family engagement goals, and opportunities

> Eligibility requirements

> A summary of what the program offers families and children of different ages

> A few photos of the entrance and classrooms for different age groups

> Photos of the staff—teachers and others they may not have met—and their names and titles

When families visit several programs, this information may help them remember each program and the people who work at each one.

Later, when families review the packet, the handouts and photos will help them recall their visit and consider whether your program is a good fit for them and their child. They can identify similarities and differences between their goals for children and those addressed in your program.

4. Begin Getting to Know Each Other

When you meet with a family, break the ice by sharing information about yourself. For example, you might talk about your interests (running, salsa dancing, raising dachshunds, reading, going to the movies), use a photo to introduce your own family, and describe how you prepared to be an early childhood educator (CDA, community college, university). Photos can be particularly helpful when meeting with families whose language you do not speak. If there are bilingual members of your community who participate in welcome meetings and tours, it's a good idea to provide training to be sure they represent the program accurately. Encourage these individuals to share a bit about themselves and clearly express the overall goal of the meeting: building a relationship with the family.

Be sure to ask about the family's home life, culture, preferred languages, what drew them to the program, and what they expect an early childhood setting can offer their child and themselves. In casual settings, it's easy to relax and share information, so keep the discussion conversational rather than following a list of questions or a script. While talking, think of ways to bring the child's unique characteristics into the conversation. This means asking about something the child likes to do, or something you notice about the child (Brazelton & Sparrow 2006). Upon learning that Lyla's favorite dish is beans and rice, her teacher tells her parent, "That's good to know. We serve that for lunch several times a month."

5. Summarize, Take a Tour, and Explain Next Steps

Review what was discussed in the meeting and explain the next steps for families if they decide to enroll their child. For example, they might be placed on a waiting list or have to meet certain financial requirements to be eligible for the program.

Invite the family to take a tour of the program—especially the classrooms. Ask a current family to give the visiting family a tour, providing a parent's perspective. Develop a written guide for parents who give tours, with simple bullet points and photos. Parents can highlight their own experience, and the prospective family can take notes using a simple checklist as they tour. *Selecting Quality Care: A Parent's Guide*, which is available online from the Oklahoma Commission for Human Services, includes an example of a checklist for program tours.

After the tour, ask the family if they have any additional questions. Answer these on the spot or promise to contact them soon if you need to do some research. A former teacher, now parent, says, "My preschool colleagues and I could have more thoughtfully eased transitions if we had supported the parents as attentively as we supported the children" (Valente 2018, 7).

6. Convey Your Genuine Appreciation

Thank the family for making time to meet with you. Let them know it was a pleasure to get to know them. Walk them to the exit, offer thanks again, and remind them to feel free to contact you by phone or email if they have questions or once they have made a decision. Remind them that answers to some of their questions may be in the welcome packet.

7. Reflect on the Visit

There is much to learn about a family that you will not find out in that first meeting. Some families are open and eager to share information about themselves, while others are more reticent. You may encounter families who display signs that they might be experiencing stress or trauma. Some parents may seem rushed or shy or tense or even a bit rude. One of the keys to beginning a trusting relationship is to accept that there are reasons for the way families behave that you may not immediately understand. "Assume the best" can be your motto. Consider what is on a parent's mind. They might be worried about losing their job because they haven't been able to secure appropriate child care. It might be hard for some families to sit and have a pleasant conversation with you if they are about to lose their home or in the middle of some other family crisis. Some families are fearful of trusting their child's care to unfamiliar people in a new setting. You may meet a family whose child has been expelled or rejected from other settings. It is important to recognize that there is some element of difficulty and stress in the lives of every family trying to balance work, home, and school needs. The kindness and acceptance you show in that first meeting can help that family more than you might realize.

Begin Relationships by Reducing Barriers

From the beginning, relationships with families depend on your ability to set aside assumptions and to be open to learning about each person as an individual. Bias can be a significant barrier to getting to know someone new. Biases influence thoughts and actions with feelings either for or against something. Bias is built on assumptions you may or may not be aware of. The latter, *implicit bias*, happens when individuals are not aware of their biases, yet these barriers affect how they act and interact. Bias is part of the way humans think, but we can all strive to be more aware of the role bias plays in communications with family members (McKnight et al. 2017). Teachers might find that their views about good parenting versus bad parenting are biased. For example, in the United States, many families expect their children to become *independent* eaters as early as possible. Spoon-feeding is for babies only. But in other countries—e.g., Mexico—many adults expect to spoon-feed children into their third or fourth year, and some parents may leave work to come to preschool at lunchtime to make sure their child is properly fed. You and the child's family may think other practices are wrong or bad because they do not support the cultural goals you or the family have for the child's development. Of course, there is no real evidence either way. Children in all countries grow up to eat independently and do not seem harmed by either approach.

How can teachers begin to recognize differences without making judgments rooted in bias? This is not an easy question to answer. There will be times when a family describes a practice as "part of our culture," and the teacher recognizes that it really is unsafe or against regulations and must not be allowed at the program. It is important to be very clear where to draw the line between different and unacceptable. A helpful resource to support your reflections and actions is found in the NAEYC Code of Ethical Conduct and Statement of Commitment (2016), which includes the following Principle related to how ethical educators determine what is best for children. It says,

> P-1.1—Above all, we shall not harm children. We shall not participate in practices that are emotionally damaging, physically harmful, disrespectful, degrading, dangerous, exploitative, or intimidating to children. *This principle has precedence over all others in this Code.* (3)

One way to address bias in your thinking or in policies is to look at data and trends.

> ❯ Are children from some population groups more (or less) to be referred for special education services? For example, teachers in an urban New Jersey district-based preschool were less likely to refer children from families who speak languages other than English because they were hesitant to "label" a child when there are no screening tools in the child's home language. This practice could result in a delay in the child getting needed services.

> ❯ Do the children who are commonly found to have "challenging behaviors" share certain characteristics, such as gender or race? The US Department of Health and Human Services (DHHS) and the US Department of Education (DOE) Policy Statement on Expulsion and Suspension Policies in Early Childhood Settings (2017) reports that Black boys are far more likely to be recommended for expulsion from preschool programs than other population groups, even though they represent a smaller percentage of preschool population groups.

> ❯ Are children from certain neighborhoods assumed to be more (or less) problematic? For example, in one school district, staff thoughtlessly referred to what they called "problem children" by their bus route numbers. A teacher might say, "That child drives me crazy—he must be a Route 7 kid," to indicate the neighborhood where the child lived.

Not all examples of bias are obvious. The more all educators talk openly about possible assumptions and share our feelings when we detect bias, the more informed we can all be in overcoming bias (McKnight et al. 2017).

Learn About Families' Home Languages and Literacy Practices

Many early childhood programs in the United States include children and families who speak a variety of languages. English is only one of the languages teachers might hear and use in their daily work. A respectful and user-friendly home language survey can help all staff learn which languages families use and their skill levels in each one.

Most states require or suggest use of a home language survey, but these documents are generally not designed to provide the full and detailed information teachers need to understand each child's complex background, abilities, and needs. To start, the program can translate its forms into the different languages spoken by families. It is also important to have conversations to answer the survey questions, especially when families speak but do not write in their home language. Often teachers lead these conversations. In these cases, seeking the assistance of a translator will make the conversation go more smoothly. Using a translator tells a family that you are eager to hear the information they will share. Families who are not familiar with American school practices may see paper forms as institutional and impersonal. They may worry about answering truthfully about their home languages or about the child's experiences because they are concerned that their responses might influence how you treat their child. They might also worry about how the information will be used and may fear it will be shared with immigration authorities. Person-to-person chats help you get to know all families and begin to build important bonds. The information you learn will help teachers support individual children and engage their families. Here are some questions to guide your conversations with families.

About the child

> What is the first language your child learned?

> What language does your child speak most often?

> What other languages does he or she speak?

> When and with whom does he or she speak them?

> How often is your child read to each week? In what languages?

> What are your child's favorite stories?

> What are your child's favorite topics of conversation?

> What foods does he or she eat often?

> Does he or she help cook any of these foods?

> What does your child like do at home with his or her siblings?

> What does he or she like to do with adults in the family?

> What are some of the songs your child likes to sing? In what language?

> What does your child enjoy watching on TV? How often?

> What does your child enjoy doing on a smartphone, tablet, or computer?

> Do people outside the family understand most of what the child says?

> Do you have any questions or concerns about your child?

About the child's family

> What does your family enjoy doing on weekends?

> Would you like to talk about your community of faith? Your religious traditions?

> Which family members spend time with the child? What language(s) do they speak? In what language(s) do they wish to receive written communication from me?

Participate in the Enrollment Process

After their initial inquiry and a visit to the program, families may need some time to consider the options. When they do choose your program, the enrollment process begins. For whomever responds to the enrollment inquiry—the program director, a teacher, or an administrative assistant—it is helpful to have at hand a list of the information needed for enrollment, which could be listed on your program's website. Review and explain what documentation the family will need to provide (e.g., the child's health records). You can offer to send forms as email attachments or by mail.

In some programs, such as in Head Start, families must meet certain income requirements that require verification. Provide a simple handout, in the appropriate home language, listing what they need to bring to the program.

Many programs create enrollment packets to provide basic information for families. This information is in addition to the welcome packet provided during the visit to the program. In a few pages, you can share more detailed information about the program philosophy, policies, staff, and daily operations. The enrollment packet might also address eligibility requirements and include forms and instructions for completing them. As Chapter 3 will cover, the contents and tone of the enrollment packet are part of your family engagement system. As with other written materials, it should be available in home languages and in English.

Keep in mind how you feel when you receive a lot of important information. It can be overwhelming. Family members may have different literacy levels or may speak a language other than English. Or the information, while clear and useful, can raise additional questions or even concerns. To make information friendly and accessible to all, use simple language, short sentences, and images or graphics to support understanding. It's best to reduce the information to the absolute necessities.

Read more about the Perez family below.

> After looking at other settings, the Perez family decides to enroll 1-year-old Lina In the Creative Discoveries Early Head Start Program. Lina's abuela has been caring for her granddaughter and thinks Creative Discoveries will be a great place for her to grow and learn. Lina, her parents, and her abuela come to an enrollment meeting where each staff member expresses their excitement about Lina and her family joining the program. Mr. and Mrs. Perez talk about Lina's health and developmental history and share their concerns about supporting her learning and growth. The program director reassures the family that the staff will partner with Lina's family. The family completes the paperwork and takes a tour of Lina's classroom. Before leaving, the teacher snaps a picture of the family and one of Lina to be posted in the classroom. Mrs. Perez takes a photo of the teacher and the classroom to use when talking with Lina about her transition. As the family leaves, the teacher, Mr. A.J., says, "Good-bye for now. We look forward to seeing Lina soon."

Support Transitions to the Program

Life is filled with transitions—opportunities to bridge a previous experience with a new one. Young children and families experience transitions as the child enters the program, moves within the program, goes to a new setting, and makes the daily transition from a family member's care to that provided by teachers. Planning to ensure that young children's transitions are successful benefits families, children, and staff. By experiencing successful transitions, families can use these successful practices once they leave the program to support their child's future transitions.

Entering the Program

Ideally, when a child enters the program the transition should take place slowly, over time, while keeping the child and family at the center of the experience. For most young children, their first major transition is from home to attending an early childhood setting in which adults other than their families will care for them. This may be a child's first time away from their family, so both the family and the child need to adjust to the new people, setting, and experiences. Older children may appear eager to start "school," not fully realizing that they will miss their family. In fact, some children do well for a week or two, then experience anxiety when separating from their family. In all classrooms, regardless of the age group, it helps to have photos of family members posted where the children can see and reach them. For crawling infants, photos might be posted very low on the wall, and for older children they can be at eye level. Individual family photo albums can also help children adjust. You can help children "check in" with their families by visiting the photos, making a pretend phone call, or talking about when the family member will return.

Guide families through each step in the transition process so they and their child can settle in and benefit from the program. For infants especially, be sure to listen to families and use their suggested approaches to calming, feeding, changing, and caring for their child. These are practices they have already used at home and they know they work. Plus, infants will have a smoother transition if everyone uses the same approach.

In the following example, the Perez family and Lina transition to the program.

On Lina's first day, the Perez family arrives at the classroom where they are greeted warmly by the teacher. Mr. A.J. helps them go through the arrival routine:

1. Remove shoes when entering and use the slippers provided to keep the classroom environment sanitary for the crawling infants.

2. Wash hands—yours and your child's.

3. Store Lina's bag and belongings in her cubby (the one with the photo of Lina and her family).

Both parents see Lina's happy face in the photo, take in a deep breath, and smile at the teacher. He explains that a video of the arrival routine is posted on the program's website. Families can view it with their child and talk about it in their home language so everyone is clear and confident about what happens.

Because this is Lina's first day, the family will stay with her for a few hours. This supported transition helps everyone get used to the new daily routine.

Mr. A.J. escorts them to a table where they enjoy a family-style breakfast, with Lina seated in a low chair next to her parents. After breakfast, he asks them to remove their plates from the table and wash their hands and Lina's. The family watches the older children scrape their plates and place them in the dish pan. They smile, thinking, "One day, Lina will be doing that too."

After breakfast, the family moves to the reading area where a few children, including Lina, gather for morning reading time. The family joins in, and Mr. A.J. captures pictures of them as they read to Lina. He promises to email the photos to share with Lina.

This is the end of Lina's first day at the Creative Discoveries Early Head Start program. She and her family say good-bye to Mr. A.J. The family now knows more about a typical day, and Lina and Mr. A.J. know more about each other. Tomorrow the Perez family will leave Lina with a caring professional who has the knowledge and skills to help her feel secure as she grows and learns.

Staggering Start Dates for Program Entry

Some early education programs offer staggered start dates for young children. This strategy can accommodate the number of family members who will participate and ensure the children are not overwhelmed by meeting all their peers at one time. So, for example, one-third of the children might start the first week attending only Monday and Wednesday, one-third start with Tuesday and Thursday, and the rest start on Friday and Monday of the next week. The whole group then starts coming together as a full-time class in the second or third week of school.

When planning for a staggered entry, it is important to give families plenty of notice. There may be situations in which this kind of gradual entry is very difficult or simply not possible because of the family's work schedules or younger children who need care. What are creative alternatives? Perhaps the program stays open one evening and a few children and a teacher briefly introduce some of the classroom routines. The main consideration to gauge is how well the child is transitioning into the classroom. A child can do well the first few days because everything is new and interesting, then on the fourth day have a difficult time. Be willing to slow down the transition to ensure children and families are transitioning with ease.

Welcoming a New Family: Two Perspectives on Becoming Partners

Having a new baby is a life-changing event; leaving that baby to be cared for by others is challenging for most families. Parents need to feel confident that program staff hear and respond to their concerns, and staff need to balance these concerns with the needs of the group. Thoughtful, knowledgeable administrators, coupled with educated staff and good communication systems, can make those first few months of child care go smoothly for babies and families.

A TEACHER'S PERSPECTIVE

Caitlin works at a child care program in Maine. She has been caring for babies and engaging their families for more than 10 years. She says:

Valerie and Dan are first-time parents. Valerie was about eight months pregnant when they first visited the center. I would be their child's first caregiver and, understandably, they had a lot of questions. Valerie asked if I would be the one caring for her child or if it would be another caregiver in the room. I explained that we assign children to specific caregivers so the child and the family has one person who fully understands the child's needs and the needs of the family. As the person who will care for their baby, I will perform most routines—like feeding, changing, and napping—until he gets to know and trust me. Then as he settles in, different caregivers may carry out some routines when I am busy with other children. We work as a team to respond to babies whenever they need something.

When Dan asked about my schedule, I explained that I work three days a week from 7 a.m. to 3 p.m., and then two days a week from 10 a.m. to 6 p.m. This allows me to see the family and the child at different times of the day. I asked Dan if he had any questions, and he wondered if he would be able to visit during the day. They live close by, and Dan works from home. I described our open-door policy, so he can visit at any time. I also shared that they can call at any time and reach me through an online connection. I described our Real Time app, where we post photos, observations, and routine care procedures that families can access at any time. I also asked if they could bring photos of important family members and explained that we display them in the room to help bridge the gap between home and the program.

One of my goals during meetings such as this one is to let the family know that our relationship is a partnership and that communicating regularly is essential, especially at the start and at the end of each day. I remember what I needed from my child's caregiver when she started child care—know my child, appreciate her uniqueness, and support me when I'm unsure or have questions. This is what I try to give each family. At the end of our meeting, I explained that after their baby is born they can visit the center a few times and spend an hour or two getting a sense of how the day goes.

A few months later, Valerie and Dan returned with their son, Luke. He is a beautiful baby, and they are proud and exhausted new parents! Luke is still waking up a lot at night. Nursing was hard for Valerie at first, but now it's getting better. Dan is thrilled to be a dad but shared that he had not expected some of the challenges they have faced. He sees that things are beginning to get a little easier. They came back the following week and stayed for another hour and looked more relaxed by the time they left. Valerie works at the hospital across the street, so I encouraged her to come by whenever she wanted. She lets me know when she will be coming to nurse Luke and when she is running late. We discussed his current routine, how they help him fall asleep, and how many ounces of breastmilk he typically takes from a bottle.

When Luke was just shy of 3 months, he joined our group. Valerie dropped him off, and I told her to give me a call if she had any questions or just wanted to know how he was doing. She came back at noon that day and nursed him. I was able to get him to wait for her to feed, but on the third day she was a little late and Luke was getting upset. I gave him some milk to hold him over until she arrived. When Valerie came in I explained that Luke had been fussy, so I gave him an ounce to hold him off. This practice also lets Luke trust that we will meet his needs. She seemed to understand.

In the next few weeks, Valerie had lots of questions and some concerns, as many first-time parents do. It's my job to put them at ease by listening carefuly, answering their questions, and asking for their ideas about how best to care for their child. I try to make the program fit the child as much as possible and not make the child adapt to the program. Valerie was concerned about Luke sleeping in the vibrating seat; she doesn't use that at home and usually rocks or nurses him to sleep. I explained that we use them once a baby is fed and changed so we can attend to the other babies who need us. As he gets older and his naps get longer, he will nap in his assigned crib.

Dan picks up Luke a few times a week. One day he shared that he reads to Luke at home and asked if we read to the babies. I explained, "When babies are awake and alert, we read to them or they look through board books." This is part of our end-of-the-day routine when babies are waiting for pick-up and, as babies go home, the group size shrinks.

Dan also said, "Luke's pediatrician asked us to put Luke on his tummy more, but he doesn't seem to be pushing up with his arms at home and gets tired quickly. Have you noticed a similar behavior?" I said, "We do put babies on their tummies when they are awake," and added that sometimes big babies like Luke need a little support. I showed him how we roll a blanket and place it underneath Luke to help him support himself. Dan really liked that strategy and said he would try it at home.

THROUGH THE EYES OF THE FAMILY

Valerie and Dan are first-time parents of baby Luke. Valerie shares their story.

When I got pregnant we were both so excited. I had heard that the child care program associated with the hospital where I work was very good and an NAEYC-accredited program. We visited the center and put our names on a waiting list for late September. Baby Luke arrived as expected in July, and I planned to return to work at the end of September; Dan would have a few weeks off before he returned to work. My first few months as a mother were much harder than I or Dan had anticipated.

Our son had a tongue tie that caused problems with latching and led to problems with nursing. Dan was extremely supportive, but it was really hard for him to watch me struggle and to see Luke struggling, too. I felt overwhelmed and exhausted most of the time and not like myself at all. When it came time to return to work, I was ready. We both visited the center and met Caitlin and thought she was awesome. She answered our questions and was open to our suggestions. We both agreed Luke would be comfortable with her and in the program.

We revisited the program a few times after Luke was born and continued to think we had found a good place for Luke. The first day I dropped him off, though, was stressful. Caitlin was great, and Luke was fine, but when I went back to my desk I just cried. I wondered, "How could I let someone else care for my baby!" It really helped that I could visit during the day and nurse Luke. Dan went by several times that first week and visited with Luke, too. It got easier as the week went on. The center's app was easy to use, and we enjoyed seeing photos of Luke during the day. Caitlin posted lots of information about how she was caring for Luke and how he was responding. These updates helped to put us at ease.

Each morning and evening we exchanged information with Caitlin about Luke's routines and activities. If Caitlin wasn't there, she left a detailed account of his day that the other caregiver shared with us. We felt supported and reassured.

Nevertheless, we struggled with some things. For example, the center uses chairs that vibrate, and we have never liked that kind of stimulation for a baby. We prefer to hold him and rock or nurse him to sleep. But it made sense that when people are caring for four babies at a time that this type of equipment would help meet a baby's needs promptly. We also worried that they were feeding him too much or not enough or not keeping to the schedule we thought was working well. Lots of worries were eased by the open and consistent communication that Caitlin cultivated. Still, the first month was hard.

Now Luke is 6 months old and thriving. He's beginning to sit on his own, nap more regularly, and most importantly sleep through the night. Sleep has made the biggest difference for us! Caitlin continues to update us daily, and we are less worried than in the beginning. Luke smiles when he sees her, and we know that he is in good hands!

Note: Thank you to Linda Gillespie for sharing this story.

Conduct Home Visits

In many programs, after the enrollment process is completed, home visits are a next step. They take place before the start of the program year or soon after a child and family enroll in the program. In some programs, home visits are repeated about halfway through the year. Home visits are opportunities for teachers and families to get to know each other in the child's home setting. The child and family are the hosts. This visit is a time to begin to understand how this family's day-to-day home life might influence their child's development and learning and to determine the best ways to form a reciprocal partnership with the family, which supports the third principle of family engagement: "Programs and teachers engage families in ways that are truly reciprocal" (NAEYC, n.d.). Teachers will learn more about the people, activities, books, and materials that fill the child's early experiences. Using this information, teachers can build important home–program connections that help the child learn.

Home visits—for new and currently enrolled families—are opportunities to exchange information and build rapport. They are scheduled times when families and teachers can ask and answer questions and plan ways to support a child's progress. They also allow teachers to observe the child and family in the home environment and learn more about their culture, language, interactions, and parenting style. The dual purpose of the home visit is to extend the educational goals to the home setting and to get familiar with how the family interacts with each other.

Head Start and Early Head Start program requirements state that home visits are to be completed for all children. Typically, two teachers conduct each home visit. Many child care and preschool programs also follow this practice. While not as common, a growing number of elementary school districts have adopted this practice because of the benefits for students, families, and teachers in supporting home–school connections, increasing family engagement, and reducing chronic absences (NEA, n.d.)

If your program has guidelines for home visits, review them with the family prior to scheduling a home visit. It's important for all participants to understand the purpose of the visit. Families embrace home visits in different ways. For some families, they are honored to share who they are and welcome you with joy. For others, a home visit can be intimidating and create worry. In such instances, an alternative is to meet the family in a neighborhood park or coffee shop; a neutral location helps reduce anxiety as you begin to build the relationship. You might ask the family to bring certain items to the meeting such as photos or videos of them and their child, their child's favorite comfort item or toy, or a favorite story or song. These items will give you some insight into the child's early experiences and the home life of the family that you can use to plan responsively for the needs of that child. Consider options for families that might be temporarily homeless or sharing a residence with others, such as meeting in a library or at a community center.

In some programs teachers conduct home visits; in others, social workers or family liaisons visit families in their homes. This is an important decision. A teacher might be more focused on using the visit to look for signs about what the child is experiencing at home and how this might affect learning. Others might focus more on becoming familiar with the culture in the home or about health

Conduct Home Visits is based on content developed for a forthcoming online training program developed by the National Center on Early Childhood Development, Teaching, and Learning, Office of Head Start: Sharing the Caring with Families, Beginning Teacher Series Infant and Toddler.

An Orientation "Encyclopedia" for Children and Families

Donna King is the founding teacher of Children First, a small nonprofit part-day preschool in Durham, NC. Throughout the program's 28-year history, it has focused on helping children develop into confident and expressive individuals who are also caring and responsible participants in the community. Programming is based on the belief that young children should spend their days deeply engaged in play with each other and with materials, and that they thrive when a lot of that play happens outdoors in nature.

CHALLENGE   Our program is small—12 children and their families with two teachers—and we know it takes a collective effort to provide quality care and education. We make sure families understand that their engagement is an essential part of every family's experience here. We explain that we give a lot and will need them to give a lot, too. As explained on our website, "Every child's 'program' at Children First is different, because it grows out of the families' and teachers' shared understanding of the child's strengths, challenges, and potential. That understanding grows and evolves as families and teachers communicate about their observations, their theories, and especially their feelings and hopes for the child."

STRATEGY   Our comprehensive orientation begins when families first show interest in Children First and continues through the first day of attendance. In April of each year, children are accepted for the next school year. For each new family, we create a Welcome Book, a print and photo-illustrated "encyclopedia" of Children First. Current children help create the books, and new children and families have all summer to explore the contents together. We also ask continuing families to buddy up with a new family for a playdate so the child will begin the year with a friend. In August we hold individual meetings with incoming families. One teacher sits with family members as they share what they want us to know about their child, while the other teacher explores the environment with the child. During these meetings we also "walk" the family through the morning routine so they are prepared for their child's first day.

RESULTS   Families who enroll their children in our program understand our goals and our strategies for achieving them. They know we will spend a lot of time outdoors, that their children will tackle challenges and take physical risks, and that their children will do a lot of thinking, wondering, and theorizing. When their children come home a little dirty and filled with interesting, engaging experiences, families are not surprised because their orientation prepared them for these outcomes.

UPDATE   Our careful and structured orientation continues, with adjustments made as we learn more about what's effective. Before family conferences in October, we invite new families to reflect on their orientation experience and make suggestions. When we start the new Welcome Books in the spring, we again invite families to share: "What do you wish you had known before you started at Children First?" Those responses get incorporated into the FAQ document we share with next year's incoming families.

and safety issues. Programs typically develop a list of guidelines for observations and questions to be asked, or topics of conversation so that the home visit builds a positive relationship with the family and results in useful information for you and other team members.

Prepare for a Successful Visit

Home visits are most successful when those conducting the visit have done their homework before the visit. To begin, they can review the family's enrollment forms, needs assessment, and other information provided by the family. Here are some additional ways to plan for success.

Plan for Success

> Find out which family members will be present and participating in the visit. This might include mothers, fathers, siblings, other close relatives, partners of the parents, and other people who live in the home. The child's guardian and the child should both be present in the home for the visit. Learn everyone's names and how to correctly pronounce them.

> Let the family know the purpose of the visit before you schedule it and arrive at their home. Encourage them to think about what they want to know from you, and explain that one goal for the visit is for both you and the family to begin getting to know each other. You could provide this information in writing, through photos and simple text, or through a short video.

Learn about the Family's Culture

> Figure out who the decision makers are (it might depend on the issue)

> Who typically serves as the family representative—asking and answering questions, for example?

> Is it customary to offer food and drinks to anyone who visits their home? (If so, does your program have a policy about this?)

> Do visitors remove their shoes upon entry to the home?

> What is considered a polite greeting? For example, do you bow, shake hands, or do something else?

> What other characteristics of the family's culture might affect your visit?

> Learn about the family's home language. Does the family speak English or another home language? Will you be able to communicate, or do you need to arrange for a translator to join in the visit?

Individualize for the Family

> Does the family know about your program? For example, is a sibling already enrolled, has a sibling completed the program and moved on, are cousins or other relatives taking part in the program? Use the answer to this question to tailor the content of the home visit.

> What days and times work best for this family? Be flexible. Schedule home visits at a convenient time for the family, even if this is not during your typical work hours. Offer several alternative days and times for the visit. Keep in mind an average home visit should be 30–45 minutes in length.

> Identify exactly where the family lives, including neighborhood, street, and house or apartment number. Is there parking? Can you walk or take public transit? Discuss safety concerns with your supervisor.

> Organize and make copies of any written materials—provide these in the family's preferred language. Bring multiples of any forms and pens, in case the family does not have these on hand.

> Bring a photo album that shows what typically happens in the classroom as children play and learn together with their teachers. You can use this to give an overview of the classroom arrangement and learning centers.

Implement Your Plans During the Visit

You may feel a bit nervous visiting a family's home. The family might be nervous to have you as a guest in their home. However, if you have completed the above steps, you should feel prepared and able to put them at ease. Here are some tips:

> Once at the door, knock or ring the bell. When the family opens the door, introduce yourself and state that you have come for the home visit.

> Wait for them to invite you in and show you a seat.

> Take out the items you need for the visit such as a notebook or pad of paper and pen; your tablet, forms, and handouts; the homemade toy you brought for the child (see next bullet); and the classroom photo album.

> Introduce and leave behind an age-appropriate, inexpensive play material for the child. Choose something that will be fun and that the family could make themselves with household items, such as a puppet made from a sock or paper lunch bag. The child can use it during the visit and afterwards.

> Comment about something in the setting, as you might when visiting a friend.

> Start the conversation by explaining the purpose of the visit. Wait for a response, and then keep the conversation going. (Avoid asking too many close-ended questions.)

> Ask an open-ended question about the child and the adults, then sit back and listen to the response. Use nonverbal gestures to indicate your interest and eagerness to hear more. Some examples:

  • What does your child like to do when he or she has free time?

  • What is your child's favorite place in the neighborhood?

  • What would you like me to know about your child?

  • What would you like to tell me about your family, including any recent changes in your life that you'd like us to know about?

> Thank the family for their time and for hosting you in their home. Remind them of when you will see them again. "We'll see you next on Monday the 9th at 7:30 a.m. We're so excited you'll be joining our program!"

Follow Up After the Visit

You probably collected a lot of information and impressions during the visit. Now it's time to follow up.

> Send a thank-you note via email or regular mail. Review what you discussed and follow up on any loose ends.

> Review your notes and plan ways to build on what you learned about the child and family. For example, you might plan an activity focused on a child's special interest or reach out to a family member who expressed an interest in learning more about your program or who is interested in contributing their skills to the class or the program.

> Continue building your relationship with the family. Keep in mind that the home visit was a good start, but now you and the family must keep the partnership going.

In the process of getting to know each child and family, you will gather a lot of valuable information. When you put this information to use, you will begin to see improvements in the program, your classroom environment, and the way people communicate and relate to each other because they are heard, respected, and understood.

Provide a Contact List for All Families

One resource that families appreciate is a contact list they can use when they have questions or need to get in touch with staff. This demonstrates that you and other staff are available to receive messages, provide assistance, and handle any issues that arise. You can share it during the home visit or on the child's first day in the program. Insert the names and the phone numbers of the appropriate people on this list.
See page 39 for an example.

Reflection Questions

Now that you have read this chapter, consider the following questions:

1. Think of a time you joined a group (e.g., a book club, yoga class, or weekend basketball league) where you felt especially welcome. What do you think made you feel that way? How could you apply what you learned from that experience to your family engagement practices?

2. Choose two strategies from this chapter to share with colleagues and your supervisor. How might these strategies be adapted for your setting and the families with whom you work?

3. What are some features of your program's family engagement system that are designed to support *all* families? What might you do to make them even more effective?

Dear _____

Welcome to our school! Please store this important information in a convenient place—on your computer, in your cell phone, or taped to the inside of a kitchen cabinet.

Issue/Concern	Person to Contact (Name and Relation)	Phone Number
If your child will be absent		☐ Call ☐ Text
If your child will be late		☐ Call ☐ Text
For questions about your child's health, teeth, vision, and so on		☐ Call ☐ Text
For questions about your bill or payments		☐ Call ☐ Text
For immediate help		☐ Call ☐ Text
For help understanding a message ☐ in English ☐ in Spanish ☐ in Chinese		☐ Call ☐ Text
When you want to discuss any problem, conflict, positive comment, or concern about your child's experience at the Wonder and Learn Program		☐ Call ☐ Text

Three

Family Engagement in Action

Family engagement happens every day through your interactions and activities with individual families and groups of families. You involve parents and other family members in their child's development and learning throughout the year, not just at certain times.

Family engagement is

> Reciprocal—Both teachers and family members exchange information, skills, and teaching strategies.

> Strengths based—Family members share their talents, interests, and expertise to support their child and benefit the whole program. Teachers see parents and families from a strengths-based perspective where parents are capable, willing, and offer value to the program.

> Individualized—Families can choose from an array of options—or come up with their own—that best fit their schedules, interests, comfort levels, and skills.

> Participatory—When parents feel connected with other families and involved in the program, they are less likely to feel isolated when they face challenges and are more likely to seek help in handling parenting and other issues.

As teachers, you can suggest ideas and welcome participation from all families whether it consists of classroom visits, making play materials, planting a garden, planning events, or helping to make decisions.

Family engagement is not just a concept or a policy. Family engagement involves action. What actions will you take to engage with families? What actions will you suggest for families to do? You will find answers in this chapter as we describe strategies, actions, activities, and projects to make family engagement successful, fun, and rewarding.

Get Started: First Steps to Engage a Family

A first step after a child and family enroll in the program is to get to know the family's needs, hopes, interests, and expectations for their child's time with you. You might collect this information gradually through informal conversations, then use what you learn right away to establish a relationship that leads to discussions about how the family members would like to be involved in the program. You respect families as true partners when you ask for their input and insight on how best to interact and communicate with them. "I would like to share stories about Emily. What is the best time for you—in the morning when you drop off Emily, at the end of the day, or another time?" A respectful interaction such as this might one day lead to the family member saying, "I really can't visit during the day, but I want to be a part of Emily's learning at the program. I noticed that the photos on the cubbies are getting torn and faded. I am an amateur photographer. I could come to pick up Emily early one day and take new photos of the children. Would that be helpful?" Of course the teacher said, "Yes, we'd love for you to do that!" Soon the cubbies had new up-to-date photos of Emily and her classmates.

It may take a while for some families to share insights about their child. As the relationship between you and the family evolves, everyone begins to gain a sense of comfort and starts to contribute as a member of the community. The previous chapter described components of a program-wide family engagement plan. When thinking about the family engagement approach you plan to implement, consider these questions:

> How do I engage new families *and* returning families?

> What can I do and say to show I am a partner in supporting their child?

> What can I say and do to show that I value family input as essential for a child's success?

As a first step, create a clear picture of who the children's families are. A concrete way to do this is to take photos of each family and ask the adults to refer to the photos while introducing their family members. (Later you can post the photos in the classroom.) Using the family stories, you can connect with one aspect—perhaps a love of soccer—and develop a working relationship with them by making connections.

Family stories can be an entry to understanding what makes each family unique. They help teachers connect to what is meaningful to families. When a family shares news of an upcoming multigenerational celebration, you can be ready to welcome a child who is dropped off by extended family members who have come for the event. When you greet Ma Ma and Po Po, the child will know that you welcome her family members. Be sure to ask for a photo from the event and post it near the photos of that child and his family.

Family and Child Time

On the first Wednesday of the month, we celebrate Wacky Wednesday with an activity for children and their families. In the lobby, the warm smiles of the staff greet families who are ready to do a hands-on activity with their children. For example, on the Wednesday before Children's Day/Book Day (*Día*), the children and families read Pat Mora's book *Abuelos* and make scary but festive masks. As the children finish the activity, they eat the nutritious breakfast that the staff makes available. After breakfast, families take their children to their classrooms.

Keep the Engagement Going

At Learning to Learn Child Development Center, the teachers have been busily preparing for the first day of the year. The classrooms are clean, well-stocked, and clearly organized so children can easily choose what to do. They include items that come directly from the children's families, homes, and communities, and thus are authentic to the child. They are arranged so children and families can see themselves reflected in the environment, which includes photos and cultural artifacts that are familiar to the children.

Outside each classroom, a shelf labeled "Invitation to Learning" holds a family learning time (FLT) activity. During FLT, a family member can engage in one-on-one play with a child. The adult focuses just on that moment and that child. The staff at Learning to Learn have noticed that some parents seem to find it difficult to start playing with their child, perhaps because they've never played before. FLT is an opportunity to help parents explore, play, and learn, just as their child is doing.

If you set up similar activities in your own program, describe them and explain how and where they will be available; this information can be included in your orientation or enrollment materials, or discussed during a home visit. For families who speak a language other than English, a brief video might help them understand the purpose of and steps involved in the activity. Then, when family members see one on the shelf, they will already know what is. The invitation to the learning shelf can highlight the activity materials and encourage families to interact with their child and the materials. "Use Learning Stories to Individualize Relationships," on pages 42–43, shows an example of an FLT activity and how it might be used.

Use Learning Stories to Individualize Relationships: A Playdate FLT Leads to a Learning Story

A learning story is a snapshot of a child's day or learning experience that captures the heart and mind of the child in play. Using the following story about Joseph as a guide, what story will you write? What experience do you want to capture to investigate further? Use pictures, story dictations, photos, and children's drawings or writing that represent the experience. These items will capture the child's sense of discovery and wonder. Add your perspective to the story by inserting highlights of the day. Also ask family members to contribute to the story. For more on learning stories, see Chapter 5.

The children in the Butterflies Room are helping their teachers prepare the FLT activity for February. The focus is having a playdate with a favorite person. Teachers set up a table covered with a cloth, a vase of flowers, and a puzzle to work on together near the dramatic play area. The children sign up for a time when each child and his or her family can have a playdate.

The Thomas family joined the program last year when Joseph was 1 year old. They said they were afraid about leaving Joseph in the care of strangers, given his age, but proceeded with

enrollment. At first, Joseph had a difficult time adjusting. As the year progressed and his teacher reached out to Joseph's parents, they began to develop a relationship based on trust. His teacher, Ms. Christy, welcomed them each morning with a special greeting and listened as they spoke about Joseph's experiences at home. Ms. Christy shared news of Joseph's favorite experiences with the parents at pick-up time each day. By the end of the year, Joseph and his family were at ease and fully engaged in program activities.

Use Continuity of Care

Another strategy for keeping family engagement going is a teaching and caregiving practice known as *continuity of care*. As defined by the Program for Infant/Toddler Care (PITC), continuity of care—when a child has the same teacher for an extended period of time—results in consistent relationships between teachers and children for the first three years of life or for the length of enrollment in an early childhood program (PITC, n.d.). Continuity of care can be provided in either same-age or mixed-age group care settings. In same-age settings, the most frequently used strategies are (a) to keep a group of children in one environment and change it to fit the children's needs as they grow or (b) to move the teacher with the small primary group of children to rooms or spaces that are appropriate for the children's developing abilities (Lally, Stewart, & Greenwald 2009).

Continuity of care serves as a foundation for building relationships with families, children, and early childhood teachers (PITC, n.d.). This approach engages families in the child's initial transition to out-of-home care and leads to partnerships with teachers to best meet the child's needs. The families become active participants in the child's experiences at the program, and they partner with teachers in supporting children's development. As the child becomes a toddler, then a preschooler, and eventually moves to kindergarten, the family enters the new school ready to advocate for their child and engage with teachers and school administrators. This is a success for all—the child, family, and program. A great beginning in the early years, while the brain is developing, contributes to a child's success in elementary school (Lally & Mangione 2017). The experiences of children and families contribute to lifelong learning as children grow.

Today Ms. Christy sees Mrs. Thomas sitting by herself watching and enjoying the interaction between 2-year-old Joseph and his dad, who are laughing during their playdate. The parents' roles appear reversed, because last year Joseph responded only to his mother, and his father rarely picked him up or dropped him off. Ms. Christy takes some photos and tells both parents she will have them ready at pick-up time. As the Thomases prepare to leave, Joseph runs over to his mom, grabs her legs and says, "I love you, Mommy!" Then he darts off to play with his friends in the block area. Ms. Christy, with camera still in hand, takes a photo of Ms. Thomas's face as Joseph embraces her.

Each day Ms. Christy creates a learning story for one child. She decides that today it will be about Joseph. She creates a story titled "Highlights of My Day" and includes pictures of the FLT activity with Joseph and his dad doing the puzzle, Joseph resting at nap time, and at the center of the photos, a heart with the photo of Joseph hugging his mom. The learning story has snippets of text describing Joseph's day and a box labeled "So what's next?" where the parents can contribute to the story.

When Ms. Thomas comes to pick up Joseph, it seems that she's had a rough day and is not feeling up to par. Ms. Christy hands her a printout of the learning story. Mrs. Thomas is immediately drawn to the heart in the middle and hugs Ms. Christy, who says, "You are at the heart of Joseph's life, and I want you to know how much it matters. He's able to do the things described here because you love and encourage him." They hug again, and a smiling Joseph interrupts with "Can we go now?"

Building on Children's Interests: Family Activities Strengthen Partnerships

Jenny Levinson is a preschool teacher in the state-funded pre-K program at the Wintonbury Early Childhood Magnet School in Bloomfield, CT. This program serves 3- and 4-year-olds. Its mission is "to develop the character of young children and create a sense of wonder about their environment, culture, and world." Strong family engagement is a school-wide goal.

CHALLENGE
I want families to know that I listen to, respect, and know their children. To accomplish this goal, each year I plan unique and meaningful family activities that stem from what I learn about children's interests. One goal of these projects is to strengthen my relationships with both children and families.

STRATEGY
My observations of and interactions with children help shed light on what fascinates them. Each year it is something different—masks, lemons, maps, grandparents. One year the children were enthralled with recycling. We spent weeks bringing in recyclables from home and using them to make eco art that we displayed for families during an art show.

RESULTS
Almost every child has a family member who attended the art show. Families told me their child was eager for the day of the art show and talked about it for weeks in advance. When I talk with past families, many mention family activities such as this one. It amazes me that after many years, families still remember these activities.

UPDATE
I continue to challenge myself every year to incorporate children's interests into the family activities. I know this takes intentional planning and lots of thinking outside the box. However, I have discovered these activities are meaningful and personalized experiences for children, families, and teachers alike.

Be Patient and Persistent

There are times when a teacher's family engagement efforts do not lead to immediate success. The family may resist your suggestions, discount the information you provide, and prefer to make decisions about their child based on only their own experiences. In these instances, you may need to be persistent and try different approaches, while continuing to support the child and engage the family.

Here's an example of how patience and persistence, over time, led to a successful outcome for all.

The Williams family enrolled in the Yes We Can Program when John, their first child, was 3. As John engaged in daily experiences, the teachers saw signs of potential developmental delays. They shared their observations with the family and suggested a developmental screening. The teachers explained, "After we receive the screening results, we can work together to promote John's development and learning at home and at the program." The Williamses were apprehensive. But they had seen similar behaviors at home, so they agreed to a referral for developmental screening. The screening determined the need for further assessment to learn more about John's development and to identify the services he would need to reach his potential. The assessment results led to a diagnosis of autism. The Williamses had never heard of autism and were unsure of how to access appropriate resources for John. They decided to get services through a private therapist. When the teachers asked about how things were going, they replied, "Oh, everything is fine." They said John's behaviors were normal and nothing was wrong with him. The teachers continued to engage with the family and work with the therapist to provide appropriate services at the program. Eventually, John moved to a public preschool program where the adult–child ratios were better suited to greater individualized attention.

Soon afterward, the family enrolled their second boy, Mark, in Yes We Can and again, the teachers noted signs that are typically associated with a diagnosis of autism. They shared their observations, but the family was not concerned. They could see that the teachers met Mark's developmental needs and made classroom accommodations when needed. For example, the teachers made sure that Mark had space to play independently or with the group. Thus, Mark could be successful in his own way. With a teacher-to-child ratio of 3:8 and a lot of one-on-one guidance and assistance, Mark progressed. The teachers regularly expressed to the family that Mark would be more successful if he received special services. When it came time for Mark to transition to the 3-year-old classroom, the teachers recommended that he move to a setting with more adults and fewer children in the classroom. Mark's mom was concerned about him leaving the program, but in the teachers' view, the 3-year-old room had too many children, too few teachers, and elevated noise levels, all of which would make it hard for Mark to succeed. The family continued to believe Mark was doing fine both at the program and at home. They moved Mark to the 3-year-old room.

During the first two weeks in this new setting, Ms. Williams often stood at the classroom window, watching her son struggle. His behavior demonstrated his need for a smaller setting where he could be successful. Mark's mother talks with his former teachers, and together they planned to have him screened for services.

Throughout this process, the teachers respected the family's request to wait for services. They continued to offer them, however, hoping that the family would one day see the need. In the end, the trusting relationship between the family and the teachers led the family to accept the services that would address their child's needs. Today, the family's third son, Paul, attends the same program, and John and Mark go to public school. They both receive services at school and support at home. Ms. Williams is the liaison for the Autism Spectrum Parent Support Group—a community-based program for parents of children ages 2 to 12. She is also a leader on the parent advisory council and an avid supporter of families who struggle with their children's developmental issues.

These brothers now receive appropriate services because their teachers and family members had built a strong, reciprocal relationship over time. The teachers remained sensitive to the family's need for information and resources and patient enough to keep offering the services the children needed.

Count Men In

The information covered in this chapter is applicable to all family members of any gender. However, many programs find that they need to try different kinds of strategies to get to know and engage men who play an important role in children's lives. Some staff admit that they might not be as responsive to male family members as they are to female family members. Fathers, grandfathers, uncles, and other male family members may feel discounted or uncomfortable developing relationships with a child's teachers. As noted in Chapter 1, millennial families share certain beliefs and approaches to parenting. Two-thirds of the parents in these families do not follow traditional gender roles, one-third share chores equally, and millennial fathers see involvement to be a positive masculine trait (Gross & O'Neil Hart 2017).

Me and My Family

Debbie Walsh is a prekindergarten teacher at Green Acres School in Rockville, MD, a school that implements a progressive educational approach for children from preschool through grade 8. The school is a diverse community of families, teachers, and administrators, all encouraging children to learn by using active, hands-on teaching methods.

CHALLENGE

Our family engagement was limited to a handful of participants. In prior years, during intake conferences we asked families if they had special talents or interests to share with the class. Only a few felt comfortable sharing a talent, but we sensed that many wanted to visit the classroom. Our goal was to find a way to encourage all family members to join their child in the classroom without making anyone feel compelled to come up with an activity or an interest to share.

STRATEGY

Teachers and staff thought of ways to involve families that would respect their time, work, and other commitments and could be adapted to their comfort level. We reviewed and evaluated the effectiveness of previous ideas, such as a guest reader program, thus learning that some family members felt unskilled in reading aloud to young children. Some had younger children at home and could not find child care. Others could not make time in their schedule during pre-K morning reading time.

During the August intake conferences, families happily shared activities they enjoyed doing with their child. They introduced or talked about other family members and described cultural and family traditions, including their favorite everyday and holiday foods.

After reflecting on all the information we gathered, teachers and staff planned a yearlong program called Me and My Family. We offered each family a 15- to 30-minute time block—the beginning of the school day, lunchtime, or the end of day—to share with the class. Families could decide what to share. Other family members and even pets were invited to take part.

RESULTS

In its first year, Me and My Family had an 89 percent participation rate. During the second parent–teacher conference, families' comments were positive and several volunteered to help in other ways. Parents said the availability of numerous time slots made it easy to participate and liked the opportunity to include all family members.

During each Me and My Family visit, we took a photo and posted it in the snack area. As the photo gallery grew, so did the conversations children had during snack time. These conversations sparked further interest in learning about many kinds of food, the culture of the families, the languages children and their families spoke, favorite children's book authors, and many other topics.

UPDATE

Me and My Family has helped foster a stronger sense of community within the classroom. Children feel more comfortable interacting with other children's families during school-wide events, field trips, or even casual conversations at drop-off and pick-up times.

Breakfast Club: Enjoying Coffee and Conversations in the Morning

In 1975, Lynn A. Manfredi-Petitt and her husband, Bob Watkins, opened The Creative Comfy Day School @ Lynn's House, a family child care home in Decatur, GA, serving up to six children from ages 2½ to 4½ years old. Although they no longer provide full-day care, the program is still open for drop-in children and parents. This family child care program, like many others, emphasizes family engagement.

CHALLENGE

Drop-off times can be stressful, even in a warm family child care setting. Parents and other family members have places to go and work schedules to meet. That said, a longer drop-off transition period can ensure that children, families, and educators have a great start to the day and opportunities to build genuine relationships.

STRATEGY

Every day begins with a healthy breakfast. Often children who are early arrivers are already eating breakfast when their friends arrive. Because family members often sat down and joined us for short periods of time in the morning, we established an optional Breakfast Club so we could enjoy a relaxing time together before the adults had to leave. Some families stay for breakfast every day, while others stay when they are able to arrange their schedule accordingly.

RESULTS

Good-byes are less stressful, and children often leave the table to choose free play activities. Families can see how their children engage with materials and with each other. Family members and providers are able to observe how each guides children's table behavior and adjust accordingly, which is good for the children.

With Breakfast Club, everyone's day starts in friendly, relaxed ways. When morning circle begins, family members are ready to leave for work. They feel acknowledged and appreciated by fellow adults and have had time to enjoy their children's company. An added bonus of Breakfast Club is that parents get to know each other and form a community of support. They feel comfortable asking fellow parents to babysit when work hours run over closing times, plan playdates for their children, and arrange birthday parties. Lynn and Bob can discuss upcoming activities and gain clear buy-in from those present. Relationships are the heart of quality care. Pass it on!

UPDATE

Breakfast Club participants were amazed by the easy ways their children said good-bye and moved into their day compared to the tearful, clingy scenes that were a frequent part of previous departures. One father enjoyed Breakfast Club so much, he occasionally drops in for coffee when he can.

Early childhood programs need to plan family engagement strategies that build relationships with male family members. The following suggestions are helpful strategies to consider when interacting with all family members:

1. Learn about the relationship between the child and the family member and what this person does to support the child's development and learning.

2. Use gender-neutral language when asking for volunteers. Both male and female volunteers can repair toys, lead a cooking activity, or plan a carnival.

3. Be sensitive to the relationship between all family members, while recognizing each person's strengths and contributions to their child's development and learning.

4. Share your professional knowledge in a way that adds to, rather than takes away from, the family member's sense of competence. View every family member as capable of enhancing the child's experience the program. Look to individual strengths and discuss ways to build on them.

5. Include all family members in your communications. Make sure the mail, text, and email addresses of both parents and other family members are handy.

6. Learn about individual interests by developing a relationship with fathers and other male family members, and then include them in planning events or activities that build on their interests. Use the same approach for mothers and female family members to do the same.

7. Use the same strategies to engage fathers and male family members as used with mothers and other female family members. Sometimes men are treated like special guests instead of caring relatives who, of course, want to be involved in their child's experiences.

8. Create a welcoming environment. Include pictures and photos of men with young children as well as women with young children. Show men feeding babies and females enjoying rough-and-tumble play with toddlers and preschoolers. When male (and female) family members express an interest in a topic, post information about that topic on the family bulletin board.

9. Strive for gender balance on family committees and councils. If needed, reach out to male family members to invite their participation. (This strategy is adapted from Conducting Home Visits, a forthcoming resource from the Office of Head Start.)

For example, the family engagement activities planned by the family services coordinator of the Pittsburgh Public Schools included March DaDness, which was "designed to invite fathers and other important males in children's lives to participate in the children's early learning programs" (Saunders 2017, 29)

To learn more about engaging male family members in their children's early care and education, review the *Head Start Father Engagement Birth to Five Programming Guide* on the Head Start website. This resource includes many useful ideas for program administrators and teachers.

Create a Family Space

One way to communicate that families are a priority in your program is to designate a comfortable gathering place where families can meet and socialize with each other. The family center should be prominent, located near the entrance if possible, nicely decorated with tables and comfy chairs for sitting and interacting with educators and other parents. It's a place where it's okay to linger and talk. The family center can also be used for events such as Chat, Chai, and Coffee or Family Engagement Networking. And it can house a collection of books and other resources on child development and parenting, and resources on what the community offers families. While every family may not use the space, it is available for both casual gatherings and formal meetings.

In family child care homes and smaller programs, use creative thinking to identify where to locate a welcoming space. Two comfortable chairs in a corner, with an album of photos of the children in the program, may work. The important thing is to make this a priority. When new families appear hesitant or don't speak much English, try inviting them personally and inviting several families who speak the same language or who come from the same neighborhood to stop by on the same morning.

Offer Variety So There Is Something for Everyone

What do you know about each child's family? Many programs use a simple survey to ask parents how they want to partner with the program. (Of course, surveys should be available in all relevant languages.) You and your colleagues can review the completed surveys to learn about the families' skills and interests, and then develop a plan to work with families to put their assets to work. Family engagement is more than a bake sale or a carnival event. It's family members working alongside teachers in meaningful ways that contribute to the education of their child and provide learning opportunities for the adults as well.

Ask families to tell you verbally or in writing how they would like to be involved in the program. This is a great way to start a partnership, but it's important to engage in conversations and to ask the questions more than once. You can imagine that families might not know how to respond if they are new parents or if they've never been asked to be involved before. When a family member's skills or interests come up in later conversations, you might say, "Oh! I didn't realize you design flyers and handouts. We're having some trouble coming up with a look for our new brochure about the program. We'd love to have your input."

Parents and family members who feel needed are most likely to contribute to the program, if their schedules permit. When families are able to visit and see their child's classroom in action, they often become more confident in supporting their child's learning—now and in the future. The more contact teachers have with families who speak different languages, the easier it is to overcome language barriers. By using the following simple strategies, programs report extraordinary success engaging all families:

> Celebrate children's cultures. Invite families to share their traditions and aspects of their culture with the class. Find times of the day (group time) or places in the classroom (art area) for families to share materials from their home or to read stories aloud that reflect their culture. Arrange many opportunities, large and small, for all families to share their traditions and talents throughout the year. Schedule these events at different times and days to give every family a chance to participate.

> Offer a variety of options for family members to visit their child's classroom (not everyone is comfortable reading stories in front of a group). With a range of choices, more parents will participate with confidence. They can cuddle a fussy

baby, speak in their home language while helping toddlers plant or weed a garden, or point out sights and sounds on a neighborhood walk with preschoolers.

› Host workshops on topics the current families request rather than topics the staff or previous families think are important. Here are some ideas you can use or adapt to meet families' interests:

- Partner with a local organization to

  ◦ Offer English as a Second Language (ESL) classes. Families could learn by translating traditional stories and rhymes that you use in the classroom.

  ◦ Hold workshops on searching for a job. Cover topics such as completing applications, providing appropriate documents, going on interviews, and so on.

- Use the computers at the program to introduce families to multilingual literacy resources.

- Hold a quick and easy cooking night—provide free grocery coupons and ideas for embedding science and math learning in the kitchen.

- Plan a family game night. Provide materials for making simple games such as lotto or bingo.

- Promote literacy by sharing information about organizations such as First Book so families can build their children's home libraries at little or no cost.

› Invite family members to apply their skills and talents to enhance their child's early childhood setting. Family members, often with their child's help, could reorganize your music collection, paint bookshelves, clean and update the play foods in the dramatic play area, make or repair doll's clothes, or repair classroom books. Parents may not always believe they need your assistance, but they will usually contribute if they feel you need them! Feeling needed and valued is the best kind of motivation for family engagement.

Multigenerational Participation

At a New York City early childhood program serving a diverse group of teen moms and their children, a teacher invited parents and grandparents of the toddlers to visit the class. She asked that they each bring along a meaningful family artifact, such as a mom's beloved childhood toy or a baseball glove passed down from a grandfather to a grandchild. Family artifacts convey a sense of the history and traditional oral stories passed from generation to generation. This strategy engaged several generations in the program.

› Invite experienced parents to serve as welcoming ambassadors for new families, especially when they speak the same language.

› Ask current bilingual families to explain the family engagement options to new families who speak languages other than English.

› Link new families with current families to foster greater engagement in the program. Arrange phone chains so experienced parents can call newer families to explain events, policies, and changes to new parents. Match parents up on small teams to plan and contribute to classroom activities. Working together makes everyone feel more included and fosters that deep sense of community that is great for each child and great for the whole school (Nemeth 2018)!

› Schedule events before or after the program hours so every family has a way to join in. Some participants might bring toys home to clean and repair. Others might help by conducting online research for needed materials or resources, or by creating materials such as class photo books.

Providence Connections: Identifying What Families Need

Samantha Ellwood is the Executive Director of Providence Connections in Pittsburgh, PA. The program serves children and families through its child development and family support programs. They include children from 6 weeks to age 5 in child care and Head Start and operate after-school and summer programs for older children.

Some families receive support services through family development specialists who visit in their homes twice a month. These families are typically experiencing a crisis whether it be learning to parent, finding food or housing, or coping with life's stresses.

CHALLENGE

Many of the family members we serve are under employed. They work two or three jobs to pay the bills and thus have little flexibility in their schedules. They may want to attend workshops and other events but with scheduling difficulties, and lack of child care and transportation, they cannot.

STRATEGY

A key part of this program's history guided staff in facing this challenge. Providence Connections was founded by the Sisters of Divine Providence about 25 years ago. The sisters had operated a hospital. After selling it, they looked for another way to serve the community. They travelled from door to door in the community to find out what residents needed. They identified single mothers as those most in need and decided to found Providence Connections to offer services that would support these families.

Taking our cues from this approach to identifying needs, Providence Connections established a 12-member Parent Council to advise on family needs and to ensure that planned projects and activities would be well received and well attended. To ensure the desires of multiple audiences are heard, the Parent Council includes mothers and fathers, single parents, dual parent families, and family members who care for nieces, nephews, and grandchildren.

RESULTS

Attendance at family-focused events has increased and participants are pleased with the content and the logistics. We provide transportation and child care for families who could not attend events otherwise. Thanks to the Council's guidance, we have a better understanding of families' strengths, needs, and life experiences. We work with the Council members to ensure the effectiveness of family engagement strategies.

UPDATE

The Parent Council's work has been successful. Members continue to guide staff and evaluate planned projects. Council members serve for several years, if not longer, and often act as cheerleaders for family engagement projects they are particularly excited about. Staff appreciate the feedback offered by the Council and from program participants.

Engage Families as Decision Makers

Being involved in decision-making is another way for families to participate. Inviting families to join staff in discussing issues, solving problems, and making decisions encourages meaningful involvement in the educational community (Edwards 2016). It also provides perspectives and ideas that staff may not generate on their own. This models a reciprocal relationship between parents and teachers where each one contributes to the program in a significant way.

Include Families in Decision-Making for the Program

How does your program include families in decision-making and collaborating to set program policies and practices? At Oklahoma City Educare, family members can volunteer as a class representative, be a member of the program-wide Policy Council, or join the Education Committee to inform curriculum and school readiness goals. Family members can provide firsthand feedback on these experiences and suggest ways to improve outcomes as a program community.

For instance, along with other committee members, parents on the Education Committee review school readiness goals and child outcomes. The goals are measurable and can be tracked by programs. Parents participate based on their own experiences and look at the outcomes to determine if the goal needs to be addressed in different ways.

All Head Start programs are required to include family members on their Policy Committees and Councils to achieve this type of input. These groups participate in making important decisions about operating their child's Head Start program. Interpreters and translators are generally provided as needed.

Involving families in governance and policy requires a lot of thought and balance. Programs benefit by having strong family participation and buy-in for program changes and updates. At times, some teachers and administrators find it difficult to accept this input, and it can be challenging to manage families' input, questions, and concerns. However, to achieve the goal of full family engagement, these challenges must be navigated. Professional development can help staff understand the purpose of full family engagement and learn specific strategies that make it meaningful for all. At what levels can family members enter as contributing members of the program? How are families' voices evident in the program's practices and procedures?

Collaborate on Community-Wide Efforts

Every opportunity for people to gather, work, and jointly make decisions is an opportunity to learn about who we are as educators and families, both individually and collectively. When you work with families on a project together, you cultivate relationships as you make joint decisions. In Oklahoma City, parents, teachers, family workers, and community leaders gather in June to start planning the annual Harvest Celebration. This event was established by a parent who had attended the Possibilities program (www.possibilitiesinc.com/pip), an Oklahoma-based venture designed to strengthen families. She chose to spearhead a community-wide carnival for neighborhood families, friends, and businesses. Harvest Celebration is now a successful community event that serves 200 families. The educators and family members who participate benefit from a five-month planning period and see the result of their work manifest before their

Coffee in the Lobby: A Long-Standing Tradition for All Families

Dee Dee Parker Wright is the executive director of Jubilee JumpStart, a child development program in the diverse Adams Morgan neighborhood of Washington, DC, which serves young children ages 6 weeks to preschool. Forty-eight children are enrolled in five classes. To acknowledge children's cultural and linguistic strengths, each class is taught by one English- and one Spanish-speaking teacher. This dual language approach is a bridge for the many immigrant families whose children attend the program, and it helps honor and support the child's home language and culture.

CHALLENGE

In the first 18 months of operation, Jubilee JumpStart had three directors. When I became the director seven years ago, families were already concerned, confused, and feeling disconnected about the program. Although the program was designed to welcome and nurture families, this goal was not being addressed, much less achieved.

STRATEGY

I bought a coffee maker and table and implemented a new weekly event: Parent Coffee Hour. Every Friday morning for the first two hours of operation, we kept the coffee pot full and provided donuts or pastries in the lobby. After dropping off their children, family members could stop to chat with staff or each other or sit down for longer conversations, as appropriate.

RESULTS

Parent Coffee Hour is ingrained as a vital part of our program. It takes place every Friday, unless we are closed, in which case it is rescheduled for Thursday. Family members use the time to build supportive relationships with each other and to offer feedback, both positive and not so positive, to staff. Coaches and teachers attend as their schedules permit, and specific concerns raised by individual family members are shared with the relevant teachers. It has been vital to creating a robust community within our center.

UPDATE

While the coffee event continues as originally designed, there have been three key additions. First, we created the JumpStarter Council, a group including family members, teachers, and administrators. They meet monthly. The suggestion for establishing this group came from a coffee hour participant. Second, we periodically invite guests, often representatives from community resource organizations. These are called Espresso Shots and allow families to connect with needed services. The third addition is a more formal monthly meeting for interested families. We adjourn to a meeting room to discuss topics of interest to the families. We also use the Parent Coffee Hour to present or review written communications and also to solicit quick feedback, such as which movie to watch on Family Movie Night or voting on parent leadership.

eyes. The families contribute their expertise, ideas, and work, and see staff as contributors to the community they have created. The parents understand that their voice matters: they can approach educators and program leaders, and their views will be heard and considered. The extra benefit of this collaboration is that the parents became advocates for the program. They encourage other families to get involved and contribute volunteers and members of the policy groups.

In many programs, well-loved traditional activities like the Harvest Festival happen year after year. These events strengthen a sense of community for the current group of families. Traditions are important, as is a flexibility to envision and plan new projects and get-togethers—with maximum involvement of families. Just as each new group of children arrives with different interests, assets, and needs, new families want and need to be engaged in projects they initiate and plan, with assistance as needed. This chapter included numerous ideas for engaging *all* families. It's important to remember that only some of the suggested strategies are a good fit for the families in your program. Always begin your planning by asking families their preferences. And be sure to include families in all stages of the planning rather than just asking for volunteers when the project is already scheduled and ready to go. True engagement occurs at every step in the process.

Reflection Questions

Now that you have read this chapter, consider the following questions:

1. Think of a time when you individualized family engagement. How did you respond to families' individual interests, assets, needs, and so on?

2. Think of a family with whom you have had a rocky relationship. What did you and the family do to keep moving toward a reciprocal, meaningful relationship for all?

3. Think of a community activity that you have enjoyed. What motivated you to participate? How can you apply this self-understanding to creating family engagement options?

Four

Communicating with Families

Effective communication is a key part of interacting and engaging with children and families. It includes exchanging information using verbal, nonverbal, and written methods. True communication happens when the information is both sent and received—that is, exchanged—to ensure understanding and to build relationships.

The second principle of family engagement states

> Teachers and programs engage families in two-way communications. Strategies allow for both school- and family-initiated communication that is timely and continuous. Communication takes multiple forms and reflects each family's language preference. (NAEYC, n.d.)

Everyone in an early childhood setting participates in building relationships that ultimately promote better educational outcomes for each child (Weiss, Lopez, & Rosenberg 2010). These relationships rely on clear, honest, reciprocal communication—a key component of effective family engagement for any school or program (Halgunseth et al. 2009). Open, respectful, positive, two-way communication with families makes it possible for them to share their hopes, dreams, and concerns for their children and to determine how they want to engage in their child's learning and development.

Many factors affect the sending and receiving sides of communications, such as language similarities and differences, cultural traditions related to interactions, dialects and regional nuances of meaning, and personal communication styles. Differences in any of these can act as barriers to or supports for communicating with others. You can learn information and practice strategies to overcome barriers, use supports, and create a mutual connection between yourself and the children's families.

Effective teachers create a plan for communicating with families that considers the content and strategies that will enhance their individual relationships with each family. Such plans often reflect the goals and practices of the program's overall family engagement system. A clear focus and intentional plan helps you and families know what each partner will share and receive during communications. When communication is planned, intentional, considerate, and inclusive, family engagement can blossom.

Form a team with colleagues such as your coteacher or other teachers of the same age group and review your current approach to exchanging information with families. Working together can make your efforts easier and more effective. Follow these steps to create a Family Communication Plan.

1. Establish goals and objectives in line with the program's overall family engagement system

2. Identify the types and recipients of information to be exchanged

3. Determine how to invite and use information shared by families

4. Choose family communication formats and strategies

5. Consider ways to support diverse families

6. Ensure family–teacher communications are reciprocal

7. Address communication challenges

8. Explain emergency preparedness policies and procedures

9. Address frequency and quantity of information shared by teachers

10. Schedule periodic evaluations

Establish Goals and Objectives

Each teacher communicates with families, but that communication does not happen in isolation. When you consider everything that will be sent to the families of the children in your class, you can plan your own communication as part of an overall system. For example, you might send home only one notice—but if that notice comes on a day when the family has received a tuition bill, a health form, and a request for contact information from other parts of your program, your notice might get lost. Communication connects all parts of an early education program's efforts. When communication is functioning well, your work is more effective and more rewarding. The interactions between you and family members are the foundation for family engagement. Communication also involves the connections you make with your community, interactions with colleagues, and what you do to enhance communications between families and each other and with members of the community.

Communication Pathways

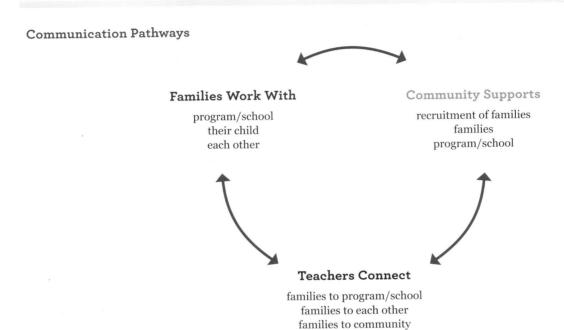

Families Work With
program/school
their child
each other

Community Supports
recruitment of families
families
program/school

Teachers Connect
families to program/school
families to each other
families to community

Sample Goals and Objectives for Family Communication

Communication Objective	Method
Encourage on-time morning drop-off so Roxanne and her dad, Jason, have a comfortable transition to begin their day.	1. Create and share a photo-illustrated book about morning activities that Roxanne won't want to miss. 2. Hold a conversation with Jason to find out why they are often late; discuss Roxanne's early morning upsets, and think of ways to address the situation. 3. Send text and/or phone messages thanking Jason for improved on-time record. 4. Talk with Roxanne, one on one, to learn what makes her comfortable at drop-off time. Let her family know you plan to make improvements in your practices to help Roxanne cope with transition times. 5. Talk with your supervisor about possible program-wide changes such as setting out coffee, fruit, and bagels to welcome families in a positive way (so Jason can grab a coffee at the program before heading to work).

Identify the Types and Recipients of Information

It's important to ensure each family gets the information they require and that they respond to provide the information you need. The table below can help you sort the types of information you might exchange with families.

Categories of Information You Might Exchange with Families

Requires Family Response	For Information Only	Action Item
❯ Permission slip	❯ Family policies	❯ Home learning activity
❯ Bill or invoice	❯ Notices	❯ Advocacy suggestions
❯ Medical form	❯ Services available in community	❯ School wish list
❯ Emergency form	❯ Child's progress report	❯ Volunteer opportunities
❯ Home language survey	❯ Screening/assessment	❯ Newsletter with objectives
❯ Invitation to event	❯ Updates on school events and experiences	❯ Intervention guidance
❯ Request for information		❯ Survey on topics for family workshops

When sharing sensitive information such as health concerns, financial information, or legal issues, carefully select the communication venue. Your choice of venue will depend on the families' needs and circumstances and the urgency of the message. For example, it would not be appropriate to ask a family member about her health problem or a late fee while standing in the hallway where others might overhear what you are discussing. Find a private location and appropriate time for this kind of conversation. This is one reason why many programs ask family members not to use their phones during drop-off or pick-up times. The person on the other end of the phone conversation might overhear confidential information or interactions with children.

Some or all families may need information about preventing and responding to illnesses, access to social services, or changes in financial circumstances. This information can be vital for families in need, but they may not always feel comfortable asking for it. For example, it may seem helpful to have brochures about coping with difficult pregnancies, but a family member might be too embarrassed to be seen picking up one of those brochures. It is not always obvious which families need certain help. An adult may suffer from depression or another seemingly invisible illness or disability. A family may seem financially secure, but a sudden setback could lead to trouble paying bills and place them in danger of losing their home. So it may not always be possible for you to know what kind of help to suggest.

You can send home brief handouts with information about the kinds of services that are available in your community, using the home languages of the families as much as possible. If your program includes a health professional, social worker, family specialist, or other individuals who can provide additional information and support for families, include their contact information in handouts that you share with families. This ensures that all families have at least been exposed to the information without making assumptions about specific families or individual family members. It's best to provide the information more than once, using more than one kind of media. In some programs, a designated staff member stays in touch with local health care and social service agencies to make sure information about available services is up to date. Helping each family receive what they need to address challenges has a positive effect on their child's development and learning. Thriving families are more likely to create home experiences that help children grow, learn, and succeed.

Teachers often share information with families via images posted on social media pages. While it may be true that "a picture is worth a 1,000 words," make sure you have written permission from a parent or guardian before posting photos of children. Families may have many reasons for refusing permission to post photos of their child on social media, especially when they are facing challenging circumstances. This is especially true when the family is undergoing a custody dispute, or if the child is in foster care. In these cases, try to take photos of activities without showing children's faces or identifying marks. For example, take photos of the child's hands playing with clay or holding a favorite book. It may be necessary to take a break from showing photos of any of the children to avoid compromising one child's situation or to avoid children feeling left out. This is one area of family communication that creates a need for new understanding as the opportunities and risks associated with social media present themselves.

Determine How to Invite and Use Information Shared by Families

This step begins with understanding that families are families, in all kinds of ways. Some ways of being a family may be familiar to you and others may be new or surprising to you. No matter who is part of a child's family, you can be sure that that child is precious to that family. This belief can be your focus. There is one thing you can always be sure of about families of young children: they do not have easygoing lives. They are likely to have many competing demands on their time as they balance the responsibilities and challenges of raising a young child with what they need to do at work and at home. When interacting with families, it is always best to approach with an open mind and an understanding heart. If your goal is to provide the best possible care and education for that child, then everything you do to relate to and support the family is another step toward reaching your goal. Consider the many different kinds of experiences and backgrounds families may have. Some of these may be clear to you as soon as you meet a family, and others might take a long time to discover and understand. How might a family's particular situation—both past and present—influence their relationships with their child? with you? their child's learning? Be open to learning about and understanding a family's experiences that contribute to both their strengths and their struggles. Be vigilant, however, about not judging families or assuming that because a family has certain experiences, the child will behave or learn in a particular way. Families and children are unique. Where there are challenges, focus on discovering ways can you support the family so the child can learn.

While individual families are unique, each family is the center of expertise about their child. Having known the child from birth (and before), they bring significant funds of knowledge about the child's development, health, and home life and experiences—all the things that make that child who he is. Young children are not yet able to express details about their culture, home language, family, and interests, so educators depend on families to help them get to know each child and keep up to date about the child's development and interests.

One Head Start teacher engages families through scrapbooking. Before the child starts in the program, the family receives a package of materials and instructions for using them to create a scrapbook that tells the child's story. This project is successful because most families enjoy making the scrapbook and are proud to send in their creations. Both teachers and families add to the book throughout the year, and the books travel with children when they transition to a new class or school. These books can be sturdy enough to stay available to children on the bookshelf or can become part of the child's portfolio file.

In a less formal example of information sharing, when a father brought his toddler to class one day, he took the time to share a few photos and video clips on his phone of the child catching a ball at home. It was a sweet moment—both the parent and the teacher were delighted to see the child's activity. It was also a helpful way of sharing information that could be used to teach and nurture that child—even if the father and teacher don't speak the same language.

"Information Families Might Share with Teachers" on page 62 highlights some information that families might share in writing, in conversations, during home visits, or through countless other interactions that occur while building and fostering a respectful relationship. After families share information with you, ask, "How might I use it to modify or individualize the program so children are successful learners?"

Information Families Might Share with Teachers

Language(s)	Culture	The Family	The Child
> Primary home language > Other languages spoken with or by others who interact with the child > Child's language skills (e.g., uses brief sentences) > Adult's literacy skills (in home language and English)	> Home country; length of time in US and your locale > Traditions and celebrations (e.g., annual festivals) > Family stories (multigenerational) > Favorite sports teams, musical groups > Religious practices > Foods, including current food favorites > Childrearing goals and practices	> Traditions (e.g., how they celebrate birthdays) > Who lives in the home (family members and others) > Significant people in the child's life > Routines and activities of daily living (e.g., meals, dressing, toileting, cooking, chores) > Bedtime practices (e.g., reading aloud) > Music the child hears at home > Pets > Use of computer, internet, tablet, and smartphone > The indoor and outdoor places where the child plays (e.g., in the living room, on the front porch, out in the yard, at the park) > The type of work that each family member does > The schools that family members attended or attend > Hobbies and talents	> Comforting toys, blanket, and caregiving practices > Favorite foods > Past experiences that caused trauma and stress > Favorite toys and books > Typical home activities > Interests > Fears > Siblings and other children in the child's life; experience playing with peers > Experiences that cause the child to feel frustrated > Everyday neighborhood experiences (e.g., waving at the trash truck driver) > Use of language; typical conversation topics > Music, art, and hobbies of the adults that the child is familiar with > Exposure to print, in the child's home language and English > Activities adults and children do together (e.g., weekly visit to farmers' market)

This list is not intended as a questionnaire. The items on this list outline some of the family knowledge and cultural assets that can help you get to know and understand the child and the family members. Some information might come up in conversations before the child enrolls, during group or individual conversations at drop-off or pick-up times, or during a brief text exchange.

Choose Family Communication Formats and Strategies

Today's families, many of whom are part of the millennial generation, are eager to communicate using a variety of print and digital formats. But families can be overwhelmed by the amount and frequency of information you send. They may feel similarly about the information the program seeks from them. Communications that get the most attention are most respectful of their time and make it clear how the family might use them.

The choice of media makes a big difference in the success of your communications. Always consider the needs and preferences of the recipients. Some teachers place a folder in each child's backpack to organize the papers to be sent home and returned. Some offer the option to send everything home on a flash drive. Many programs use family communication software or apps that move information back and forth using text messages, email updates, or digital portfolios. Ideally, offer several options so families can choose what works for them.

Consider the Pros and Cons of a Family Newsletter

One example of a widely used communication tool is a program, or individual classroom, family newsletter. Before you decide to create this labor-intensive communication tool, the first question to consider is "What information do families want to receive?" Your communications with families will be most successful when you keep their needs and interests in mind. Next, ask "What do I hope the families will do after reading the newsletter?" When communication specifically describes some kind of action, readers are more like to engage with and use the information. For example, if your weekly newsletter describes children's activities, ask yourself, "What will families do with the content?" If they and their child would benefit from discussing and reviewing the activities, state that clearly and provide a few suggested questions, ways to follow up at home, and an objective. If you don't have a clear answer to the above question, it might be time to revise the newsletter or find other ways to provide information that families can use. Examples will be described throughout this chapter.

Photo-Based Newsletters: Combining Images with Child Development Observations

Julia Luckenbill is the infant-toddler coordinator of The Center for Family Studies at the University of California, Davis, an NAEYC-accredited early childhood laboratory school serving infants, toddlers, and preschoolers and their families. One of Julia's tasks is communicating with families and providing access to information about their children and child development.

CHALLENGE

Most families—but especially those of infants and toddlers—are hungry for information about their children's daily activities, routines, and experiences. Exchanging information at drop-off and pick-up times is helpful up to a point, but often families—especially those with their first child—want more. No matter how much they trust the staff, it can be hard to share the care of their child with others. Exchanging information about feeding and toileting, plus a brief comment on a daily activity, is a good starting point, but it doesn't address families' need to know that their child is growing, developing, and learning in a high-quality, caring setting. This said, long conversations at drop-off and pick-up times are challenging due to the needs of the group as a whole.

STRATEGY

We create photo-based newsletters that depict children's experiences and progress in all domains, using both text and images. I often have my camera at hand and take a lot of photos during the day, making sure to document every child and every part of the environment over each two-week period. With these photos and running observations of the children, I create a photo-illustrated newsletter that describes what all the children have been doing and learning. I also include information about special projects such as cooking, working in our garden, and going on field trips. One section is dedicated entirely to highlighting empathetic and prosocial interactions in the toddler room, carefully selected to highlight every child. I also create hyperlinks to articles where parents can learn more about topics such as homemade books or short explanations about how we apply research to what we are doing in the classroom. Families receive the newsletters via email every other Friday.

RESULTS

Families deeply value the newsletter, sharing it with grandparents, trying out activities at home, and even purchasing gifts based on what they notice their child is interested in. Parents rarely ask for more information about what a child is doing and learning, though sometimes they write back to express their appreciation for the content.

UPDATE

We continue to create this newsletter in combination with other documentation efforts such as wall displays and posters. We also meet with the families for parent conferences and use the same photographs to tell the story of each child's growth across their time.

Look at Text Message Systems

You can take a similar approach when using protected text message systems such as Remind, Talking Points, or Class Dojo. Text messages allow you to focus on sending brief, significant bits of information. When used in moderation, these can be effective ways to encourage families to respond. Use them to emphasize the most useful actions for families and avoid flooding their phones with unnecessary messages. Some programs use texts to send reminders for payments or other obligations, but you can use them to build family engagement and home learning. Think of text messaging programs as two-way communication platforms and use relationship-building strategies like the ones suggested above for newsletters.

Five Ways to Use Text Messaging for Family Engagement

1. Extend learning: "We explored the circle shape today. Ask your child to find circle shapes at home, too."

2. Start conversations: "One way to begin a conversation with your child about her day is to ask, 'Who did you play with?' Then ask what they did together."

3. Give a positive reminder: "Our medical records are so important. Thank you to families who completed the forms already. We need all of the forms completed and returned by Friday."

4. Connect family cultures with the program: "Do you have a favorite song you sing to your child? We'd like to sing it in our classroom. Please reply if you can send us the song in an email or visit us to teach it to all of the children."

5. Build relationships: "We have new families joining us next week. Please welcome them by describing one activity your child really enjoys in my class."

Use Plain Language in Written Communications

Clear, effective communication is an important aspect of your communication plan. The guidelines from the federal government's Center for Plain Language are useful for any organization. The guidelines focus on the needs of the recipient rather than the needs of the sender so messages have the desired results. Some key recommendations (Center for Plain Language, n.d.) are:

> Use short sentences.

> Use words the reader will know (e.g., *reading and writing* is a more familiar term than *literacy*).

> Use clear verbs and active voice.

> Avoid slang or sayings that don't directly state your meaning.

> Use images that add meaning to the message.

> Use a positive tone that is not punitive or condescending.

> Leave plenty of white space rather than filling the page with print.

> Use bullet points, lists, and headings to guide the reader.

Search the internet for a "readability calculator." Many word processing programs such as Word include a readability feature along with word count and spell checker. Aim for a readability score lower than sixth grade to make information more accessible. This means using simpler words and shorter sentences.

Visit the center's website (www.centerforplainlanguage.org) for additional guidelines and helpful resources for all kinds of communications.

Avoid Communications Biases

Professional development and ongoing discussions can help you overcome possible biases and develop positive communication skills. You can learn appropriate ways to interact with people from diverse backgrounds. Here are some examples:

> Use person-first language (e.g., *child with a disability* rather than *a handicapped child*).

> Use everyday language and avoid using slang or nicknames.

> Use gender-neutral language when possible

> Treat everyone with respect.

> Listen patiently.

> If language is a barrier, consider using a translator, translation app, or phone translation service.

Tips for Writing Effective Emails

1. Use a subject line that clearly states the purpose within the first eight words. Subjects like "School update" or other general lines are less likely to be opened. A positive and respectful tone also helps ensure more emails are opened. Try something like "Children will sing at the next family meeting!"

2. Ask for a response, if it is needed, in the first line of the email.

3. Keep the message short and easy to read; remember, most people read emails on their smartphones.

4. Include images and white space to make messages easier to understand and more attractive to readers. Keep the words to a minimum for efficient communications.

5. Include links or attachments only when necessary.

6. Tell readers what you want them to do or what will happen next.

You can also identify and address bias by looking at how and what you communicate. (See pages 26–27 in Chapter 2 for additional information on bias.) For example, most programs and schools produce family handbooks outlining their rules, policies, and consequences. This is required reading for you to build a shared understanding with families. However, many people do not read the instruction manuals that come with appliances or cars. Why would you assume a busy family member will read the entire family handbook? Producing information in lengthy, written form is a kind of bias. Keep critical information in the handbook but also send it to families in short bits using email, text messages, video clips, or other methods that work for families. Above all, make sure that the number of positive messages families receive always outnumber the negative messages. Here are some examples of messages that programs send to families:

> Diverse languages and cultures enrich our lives. We welcome opportunities to learn about each family's language and culture!

> We understand that it is not always easy to pick your child up on time, but we want to respect the family time of our staff. If you arrive more than 15 minutes after pick-up time, you will owe $5 for each additional 15 minutes.

> We play outside every day so the children can experience all kinds of weather. Please dress your child to be ready for outdoor play.

> I take every child in my family child care home to get his or her own library card at the local library. If you would like to know more about the library's resources, I'll be happy to help.

> Pictures and videos of the children are adorable *and* informative! We love to see pictures from home. Please don't post pictures of any children on social media without their family's permission.

> We are partners in encouraging your child's development and learning and in responding to your family's requests. Visit or call Zair Moussa, our family support specialist, for information about local services.

> We appreciate your help with our fundraisers. Families are not required to participate.

Plan Ways to Support Diverse Families

Engaging families might be simple if you had a roadmap showing exactly how to interact with each family based on clearly identifiable cultural norms or practices. What makes your work challenging, however, is that no two families are alike. Each family's beliefs and practices are influenced by a complex interplay of traits and factors. For example, some parents are eager to hear your suggestions; others don't know why you are interfering in their life at home. Some families may listen to you but say little in response because they believe that they have no role in addressing issues that come up at the program. Some families expect to have a significant role in making decisions about their child, while others seem unprepared to be their child's advocate. This section describes aspects of diversity you might encounter. To know how to understand and respond effectively, learn as much as you can about the rich complexity of each family.

Think about when, how, and what you communicate with each family. Build relationships throughout the year so you can learn how their lives might change over time. Say, for example, a toddler in your class seems to be slow to develop language. After checking the enrollment forms, you find no information to help you understand the situation. However, in conversations with this family, you might learn that the child has a potential disability, that the child is a dual language learner (DLL), or that both may be true. Two additional factors that might impact a child's language development are stress in the child's home and living in poverty (Park, O'Toole, & Katsiaficas 2017). It can be hard to know what causes a language delay, so it's important to observe the child frequently and communicate openly with the family. Look for competent translators or high-quality translation software to overcome language barriers. Because DLLs are capable learners, try strategies you know and learn about new ones. Understanding the dynamics of the home will provide a starting place for families and teachers to build from and develop new learning opportunities.

Prepare Materials for Families with Diverse Languages

When it comes to effective communication, less is definitely more. Aim for less paper, less content, fewer words, more white space, more visual cues. Whenever possible, use icons, photos, and color-coding to help all families understand and benefit from the information you provide. For example, try color-coding key pieces. Print forms that need to be returned with a payment on green paper. Use blue paper for forms that need to be completed, signed, and returned. Use yellow to indicate materials are for adults only. Or adapt or develop a system that works for you.

The following guidelines are reprinted from the Language Castle blog, with permission from the author (Nemeth 2016):

1. Say less!

Reach out to young children who are DLLs and their families by paring down to the absolute minimum of messages and words needed to save money and time on translations.

2. Simplify.

Make translation more manageable and help those with low English literacy, too. Use short sentences, simple words.

3. Say what you mean—exactly.

Remove lingo, slang, acronyms, and idioms. Instead of "rain date" say "If it rains on Tuesday, we will meet on Wednesday," even though this uses more words.

4. Address language needs.

Use Google Translate and mobile apps like iTranslate to type words and hear them in several languages. Microsoft Word can translate typed words. None of these services is 100% accurate so do not use them for formal or legal documents. The Google Translate app lets you use the camera on your tablet to show printed documents translated before your eyes. Take a screen shot to email or print the translated document.

5. Save money.

Share translations with neighboring programs to save money. Set up documents as templates so you can just fill in names, dates, and so on.

6. Seek help from professionals.

Pay certified translators for important documents—and seek a professional with a background in education or early childhood for the closest match.

7. Verify content.

Have at least two readers verify content before using. Remember, not all bilingual people are suitable translators. Some may speak but not write the language. Does the content match the dialects and reading levels of your audience?

8. Review content.

Invite family members, staff, and volunteers to serve as reviewers of all materials purchased or translated. Ask them to check for both accuracy and cultural appropriateness.

9. Use repetition.

Try to use the same sentences over and over. Keep the translations and reuse the sentences where possible. Identify key messages with predictable colors or icons.

10. Use all available media.

For critical messages, ask volunteers to say messages to families in person or to call them directly to make sure they receive and understand the message. Also, it may be necessary to use email and text messages, and add pictures to ensure understanding.

As part of your communication plan, make a list of translation services, documents that may already be available in different languages, helpful videos, free guides for families, and family and staff who are members of the early education community who can help families understand key information.

Ensure Family–Teacher Communications are Reciprocal

Family communication should emphasize the exchange of information—a process in which each member of the partnership shares and receives knowledge. Effective family engagement approaches include ways to listen to all families and to each family. One step in establishing trusting, two-way relationships with families is to ask them what they want to contribute to and gain from their child's early learning setting. This simple, effective step is often overlooked. You can get so caught up in thinking about what you *think* families need or want to know that you may forget to ask them directly. The next step in establishing this two-way process is to respond to families' requests. For example, you might ask families when it would be convenient for them to attend informative workshops. You might be surprised to learn most families prefer a weekend day rather than a weeknight. It may not have been your plan to offer workshops on weekends, but once you have offered that option, you will need to give it a try. Getting to know families takes time, but investing in this process helps you respond more successfully to each family—addressing needs, responding to interests, and appreciating their language and culture. Customized communications build strong relationships and enhance your teaching, as well.

In a small study, Nicole Edwards found that families of preschoolers preferred to have an anonymous way to provide feedback to their child's teacher and program, and that teachers and staff needed dedicated time to reflect on the suggestions they received and to make plans to respond directly and explicitly (Edwards 2018). Consider these questions while planning:

> Are the families included in making decisions at the classroom and program levels?

> Is the information clearly and respectfully communicated?

> Do families know when they need to respond and how to respond?

> Is there an email address families can use to share feelings, ask questions, and make suggestions? Is this service also available via voicemail?

> How do families provide input at face-to-face meetings and during video or phone calls?

Thinking in terms of these questions helps to avoid falling into patterns and making assumptions about what families need. Keep careful records of how you send and receive information from families so you can build on what works and so you can add new methods if you notice some families are not participating.

Effective communication is reciprocal, so it builds your partnerships with families and benefits everyone. "Supporting parents' efforts to help their children develop during the preschool years improves child school readiness, reduces child behavior problems, enhances child social skills, and promotes academic success" (Bierman, Morris, & Abenavoli 2017, 2). For example:

> *Teachers* identify each child's abilities, needs, and interests, which they can use to individualize the program so every child can develop and learn.

> *Families* learn more about their child's developmental and educational experiences and can apply this information when supporting their child's learning and development at home.

> *Children* benefit from an individualized environment, materials, curriculum, and interactions that result from this exchange of information (Barrueco, Smith, & Stephens 2016).

The most important benefit of effective communication, though, is the relationships that develop between you and family members. The effectiveness of the network supporting each child's growth, development, and learning relies on the strength of these two-way relationships.

Address Communication Challenges

For a variety of reasons, many educators struggle with family communication. One critical stumbling block is the sender's or receiver's misunderstanding of the goals and content of the communication. Taking time to reflect on the purpose or intended result for a particular communication can result in improvements that work for everyone. The graphic below highlights these aims and the need to be clear about your purpose.

What Do I Hope to Learn?

Purpose of Communication

Receiver of Communication

What You Want Families to Know

"Kindergarten round-up meetings start in April."

What Families Want You to Know

"My child is allergic to all dairy products."

What Families Want to Know About the Program

"How do you celebrate children's birthdays?"

What the Program Wants to Know About Families

"What times do you prefer for family–teacher conferences?"

Teachers and other program staff disseminate or seek information because they have a particular need to know or tell families something. Make sure families understand what information you need and why you need it. For example, the program may need to complete certain forms to qualify for funding or you may need to tell families about a change in policy. Other kinds of information are responses to a family member's request or stated interest. One thing is certain: adults respond much better to information that meets their needs (Knowles, Holton, & Swanson 2005).

Another variable is the level of reciprocity embedded in the communication system. In other words, do you respond as quickly and accurately to family inquiries as you expect families to respond to your requests? Building trusting relationships can only succeed if both families and educators trust each other to be responsive and respectful. If you want families to listen to you, it is important to listen to them as well. If you want families to follow through with promises and obligations, make sure you do the same.

It is crucial to tailor expectations and strategies to meet the characteristics of each family. Research has shown, for example, that the kinds of communications and engagement strategies used to support families who are highly vulnerable must be more intensive and extensive than the methods used with other families. Families living under the stress of poverty, for example, may experience a variety of factors that interfere with their ability to participate in their child's early education activities, but additional efforts to work with them and accommodate them can lead to improvements in the child's learning (Bierman, Morris, & Abenavoli 2017).

Communicating with families who are experiencing stress and trauma may require creative options. A brief text allows you to share information they can use: "Janine tried yogurt today and liked it." During a crisis, if it is possible, a quick visit in a hospital waiting room can assure them that their child is doing well. In these instances, you can take advantage of opportunities to touch base at different times and using different methods. Phone calls, emails, paper mail, text messages, and voice messages may all serve a purpose.

Work with Families to Address Concerns

As you learn about families, and they learn about you, you will each come to trust the other person's suggestions. In addition, families will be more likely to take advantage of what the program offers. In the following vignette, the Jones family builds a strong, reciprocal relationship with their child's teacher and the program liaison. This relationship is already well-established when Kara exhibits some behavior challenges. Using a team approach, the parents and teachers work with the family to help Kara.

> When Mr. and Mrs. Jones arrive at the program to enroll their daughter, Kara, they explain, "Kara's grandmother will be picking her up on Tuesdays, but she may need to come an hour earlier than we usually do." The director, Ms. Hinman, responds, "Thank you for letting me know. We'll be glad to work with you on that schedule. I'll ask Kara's teacher to make a note of that in her weekly routine." On the first day they meet Kara's teacher, Ms. Genoa.

> Kara, now 2, is experiencing some challenges in behavior. Ms. Genoa asks the family to meet with her and her coteacher to discuss their concerns, learn what the family has noticed at home, and jointly plan ways to help Kara. The teachers share their observations that point to Kara having somewhat limited language skills that hinder her ability to express her feelings to classmates. In these situations, Kara resorts to acting out and using aggression to communicate what she wants or needs. Her parents say they have seen similar behavior when Kara plays with her cousins.

> Ms. Genoa suggests that Kara may need further assessment to determine what she needs to ensure her success. The family agrees to the assessment. As suspected by the teachers, the results point to a language delay.

> Moving forward a few months, Kara is receiving speech therapy and rapidly learning new words. She has fewer outbursts due to frustration at not being able to express herself. Her behavior issues have resolved. One day, when entering the building, the director notices Mrs. Jones talking with Kara, asking questions and smiling. What led to the turnaround? Kara's language skills improved, in part, because her teachers and parents worked together.

> Kara's road to progress and learning appropriate behaviors came about in part through the efforts of observant teachers. It is worth it for staff to spend time on establishing relationships with families. This is just one story of many that demonstrate how relationships are essential to engaging families.

Handle Conflicts When They Arise

Regardless of careful planning and good intentions, as you and families build relationships and establish lines of communication, conflicts may arise. Often these are due to a lack of understanding of background, language, or beliefs. There are generally two goals in dealing with conflict. You might focus on (a) ending the disagreement or (b) preserving the relationship (Gonzalez-Mena 2013). In both cases, good communication is essential and will lead to positive results.

When the language, culture, and other characteristics of your community change, you may need to alter the policies, rules, and assumptions that were appropriate in the past. With your colleagues, review the program's expectations for families. Establish which policies are necessary, which are in place just because "it's always been that way," and which may just be based on preferences or personal taste. Consider these examples:

> At the Happy Days child development program, teachers call each child by the name on his or her birth certificate. At other programs in the area, staff ask families what name they prefer to be used for their child. The staff at Happy Days plan to review the history and reasons for their policy and whether it is necessary.

> All the pre-K programs in Weatherville allow families to choose the language to be used for their child's learning. They can select English or the family's home language. The pre-K programs in the next town support learning using the child's home language. They know that research clearly shows that supporting a child's home language helps him or her learn more effectively and progress in learning English. The Weatherville educators plan to review their policy to determine whether it is appropriate for this decision to be a family choice or a program-wide policy.

Maintaining only necessary rules and expectations is one way to reduce the possibilities of conflict with families. This approach creates a more collaborative environment for communication that increases family engagement. Keep in mind that policies are not always the best tools in the family engagement toolbox. Positive and mutually respectful relationships are more likely to result in cooperation than strict rules and consequences. Many programs experience success when they involve families in establishing or updating policies. This approach communicates a sense of respect and belonging that encourages more acceptance of the policies and expectations you develop together.

Explain Emergency Preparedness Policies and Procedures

Weather-related and other kinds of emergencies can arise while children are at the program. Emergency preparedness information is one kind of communication that must be understood by all families. One communication method or one language is generally not sufficient to ensure that everyone has received the information. Try these suggestions.

> Establish family buddies. Ask a more experienced family to connect with a new family to make sure they understand emergency procedures. The buddy can also be a familiar contact to answer any other questions a new family might have.

> Make a video of your fire drill or sheltering procedures. You and your colleagues can make it available so all families understand emergency procedures and can review them with their children.

> Simplify written policies. This helps all families to truly understand these important messages. Simplified materials are also easier to have translated in all the languages needed in your program.

> Add each family's home language to the emergency contact list. Knowing a family's home language makes it easier for authorities to communicate with families.

> Use multiple communication methods. During an emergency, use phone, text, and email messages so everyone receives information and learns about the situation.

> Create picture cues (photos or graphic icons) for specific notices. For example, a clock with a time on it can indicate the program is closing early. Use the cues in text messages to families or as visual cues to children about what is happening in an emergency.

> Go on a walking tour of the building and nearby places with families and children. Show them where you will shelter in an emergency. This is better than handing out a written policy and hoping they understand what's in it.

> Update families' emergency contact information periodically. Follow a schedule for updates and provide periodic reminders and clarifications about emergency procedures so no child or family is overlooked.

Create culturally sensitive emergency plans and information. Children and families who have experienced violence or a natural disaster may react in unexpected ways and may need additional reassurance (Nemeth 2017).

Track Frequency and Quantity of Communications with Families

Families receive a lot of information from your program. It might come from specialists, the director, coaches, the nutritionist, and so on. Families and teachers can find it difficult to keep track of what has been shared and what responses or actions are needed. To help monitor the flow and content of information, consider the following questions.

> What is your system for tracking who needs to receive information?

> How do you know what format the family prefers?

> What information has been sent? How did the family respond?

> What other information do you need to send?

With a plan in place, communications can be easier, more effective, and less overwhelming. There are so many different pieces to the communication work of early childhood programs. Getting things organized can be very rewarding. The goal to keep in mind is how communications can strengthen your relationships with families to enhance your work with young children.

Schedule Periodic Evaluations

As with any early childhood education practice, it is important to periodically assess the effectiveness of the communication methods and processes you use to inform, engage, and exchange information with families. To ensure communication is effective, you need to know:

> What do families want to know?

> What do families want you to know?

> How do you want families to respond?

> How are families responding?

> How do families want you to respond?

> How are you responding?

Family Communication Planning Checklist

✔	What to Do	What's the Status	What to Do Next
	Identify communication team		
	Establish communication goals		
	Identify types of information		
	Describe audiences		
	List languages needed		
	List media options		
	Evaluate what works		
	Address frequency and quantity of information		
	Outline emergency preparedness		
	Define staff roles and responsibilities		
	Collect resources for communication		
	Develop tracking system for all families		

The answers to these questions and others, gained through conversations, meetings, or surveys, may lead you to adjust your communication practices. One way to enhance the sending and sharing of information is to suggest actions that families can implement. Instead of planning messages based on content (e.g., dates for upcoming field trips), plan messages based on what you hope families will do (e.g., talk with their children before and after the trip). To truly engage families, consider what you hope they can do in response to your communications and how they can tell you about their interactions with their child.

How might you and your colleagues identify the types of information you send to families and receive from them? How might you work together to make your efforts more efficient and effective? Here are some questions to discuss:

> Which teachers prepare a class newsletter?

> Which teachers send information home and which do not?

> Is any of the information we distribute incorrect or inappropriate? What is the system for regularly reviewing the information shared?

> Which fundraising projects and materials are well-planned and effective; which ones are less effective?

> What health information is shared?

> What materials are available for families and visitors at the front desk?

> Which forms require some kind of response?

> What communications are sent home for information only?

> Which information is available only for people who ask for it?

> Which information goes home on paper?

> Which information goes home via text message?

> Which information goes home via email?

> How are voicemails used?

> What flyers are available; what is their purpose?

> Does the program advertise? If so, through what channels?

Hearing from families about how your communications affect them will help you improve what you send them in the future and will help families feel like valued members of the team. Teachers at a preschool in Quincy, MA, had suggestion boxes at the entrance to their classrooms, but they were rarely used by families. One teacher decided to just ask some families what they like and don't like about the information they receive and made changes accordingly.

Seek Feedback from Transitioning Families

When families are ready to transition out of your program, it is a good idea to have an exit interview. This is a common practice in many places of employment or volunteer positions.

A teacher noticed that whenever the school used their robocall service to announce a closing or provide other important information, her phone would be flooded with calls from Spanish speaking families wanting to know what it said. The teacher started typing the message into a quick text using the Remind system (www.remind.com) so each family could receive it in their preferred language.

It can be a useful way to learn from the experiences of each family in your program. During an exit interview, teachers and other staff ask a few questions to learn what aspects of your program were successful for the family and which aspects could be improved. For example,

> What did your child mention most often when sharing the details of the day?

> Which family events did you take part in? How could they be improved?

> What family events do you wish we offered?

> Have you ever contacted someone to share a concern? If so, what happened?

Add additional questions based on your specific family engagement efforts.

Without prying, ask families to share with you why they are leaving (if it is not to transition to elementary school), and what they think you should know to better serve children and families in the future. Whenever possible, close on a positive note that leaves the family feeling valued and missed. Not only will this increase the likelihood that they will recommend your program to others, but this conversation will also give you information to engage more effectively with families.

Hold Successful Family–Teacher Conferences

The Family Communication Plan will include details on the program's approach to holding family–teacher conferences. Looking at the steps to create a family communication plan on page 74, this falls into Step 2 when you identify the types and recipients of information to be exchanged and Step 3 when you determine how to invite and use communication from families. Because this is such a large topic, we have given it a separate section.

Families and teachers share a lot of information about children through daily interactions, whether in person or through emails and texts. But these interactions tend to be brief and focused on a child's experiences in the moment. It can be difficult to accurately keep track of a child's progress in this manner. Periodic, somewhat formal, organized conferences are opportunities for the family and teachers to take a look at the child's experiences, development, and learning over a period of time and to plan what they will do at home and at the program to continue supporting the child's progress.

Typically, a program holds conferences twice a year, although some programs offer a third conference when the child moves on to a new classroom. As with home visits, conference schedules are flexible, keeping the family's situation in mind. Offer several options, including daytime, evening, and weekend time slots. Generally, all teachers in a program hold conferences at the same time of year.

Families may come in to meet the teacher as a team, including grandparents, aunts, uncles, and siblings. Other families might send a nanny, a teenage child, or legal representative. In the third edition of *Ethics and the Early Childhood Educator: Using the NAEYC Code* (Feeney & Freeman 2018), Principle 2.1 states

> We shall work to create a respectful environment for and a working relationship with all families, regardless of family members' sex, race, national origin, immigration status, preferred home language, religious belief or affiliation, age, marital status/family structure, disability, or sexual orientation. (138–139)

Being open to all kinds of families and all kinds of communication without making judgments takes practice and time.

To make it easy for multiple members of the same family to attend the conference, consider coordinating with the program director to offer on-site child care.

Many of the strategies you use to welcome families at other times are applicable during conferences. For example, allow enough time for discussions, arrange the space so teachers and family members can sit side by side, plan and prepare ahead so you can make the best use of the conference time, respect cultural preferences and practices and the language spoken by families, and encourage them to share their knowledge of their child.

Part of your preparation begins as soon as the child enters your classroom. You will be collecting photos, observations, notes, checklists, work samples, and more to document the child's experiences and progress. You will share these items, typically stored in a portfolio, with families when they come for the conference. Start the conference with positive examples of the child's growth—ideally documented by the portfolio entries—but save sufficient time to discuss issues that you or the family are interested in or concerned about. Always close on a high note. Throughout the conference, communicate your pleasure in being this child's teacher. After the conference, review your notes while your memory is clear. Highlight anything you will follow up on in the coming weeks.

Family—teacher conferences support the first principle of family engagement: "Programs invite families to participate in decision-making and goal setting for their child" (NAEYC, n.d.).

Conferences are most effective for all participants when everyone knows the goals, the procedures, and the focus. This can be accomplished when families are as prepared as the teachers.

A handout for families appears on page 79. You can make and distribute copies, translated as needed, for families to use as a planning tool prior the conference.

Tips for Successful Family—Teacher Conferences

Plan for varied schedules.

> Offer lunchtime, early morning, evening, and weekend options for meetings.
> Understand that some families arrive at appointments at the scheduled time; others may have a looser interpretation of appointment times.
> Provide supervised activities for children who must accompany parents and family members.
> Meet via video chat for those who can't come to the program.

Accommodate different languages.

> Use paid or volunteer interpreters who have received training for this kind of meeting.
> Provide a meeting summary in writing, with translation as needed.
> Keep written information brief, respectful, positive, and simple.

Learn about and consider cultural norms.

> Be sensitive to each family's comfort level with eye contact and direct language. Some expect this, others prefer a more subtle, less direct engagement approach.

> Understand communication styles and preferences. Some families provide and expect a list of events or observations in exact order. Others prefer to communicate in a less linear, story-like fashion.

> Learn about expectations for participation in the conference. Some families expect to just listen, while others expect to ask questions and provide input. Awareness of body language can help you adapt to the style that will work in each situation.

Discuss different experiences.

> Always start by sharing something wonderful about each child. Include older children in the progress discussion, allowing them to share self-selected work samples.

> Be prepared to listen patiently. Families don't always know what questions to ask right away. Teachers have the most success when they listen as much as talk during family meetings.

> Find ways to interact with each family before sitting down for a formal progress report meeting so you are familiar with their communication style and cultural approach.

> Put yourself in the place of the families and try to provide them with the kind of experience you would enjoy.

Share different kinds of information.

> Include information families can use, such as recommendations for appropriate home learning activities and relevant community resources. This changes a passive listening experience to a joint planning meeting designed to celebrate and improve their child's learning experiences.

> Share examples of progress using photos, work samples, and videos.

> Plan ahead: focus on the most important information so as not to overwhelm families.

> Include information that is best discussed during a face-to-face meeting.

Reflection Questions

Now that you have read this chapter, consider the following questions:

1. Which aspects of your communications with families have been most effective? Why do you think they have worked well?

2. Which aspects of your communications with families have been the most challenging? How did you change your strategies to address the challenges?

3. When you imagine the improvements in your work with families that can happen as a result of creating a communication plan, what specific areas of your work seem most likely to improve?

It's Time for Family–Teacher Conferences

During our family–teacher conference, we will

1. Focus on your child.

2. Stick to the schedule so every family has enough time to discuss their child.

3. Summarize your child's progress and plan for the future.

4. Listen before responding.

5. Ask your questions.

We hope you will

1. Share information with us. You know your child better than anyone else, and we will be better teachers if you tell us what you know. Think about these questions:

   › What do you want us to know about your child's personality, challenges, friends and relatives, interests, and skills?

   › What kinds of things do you do as a family?

   › How do the siblings get along?

   › How do you help your child learn to behave in positive ways?

   › What are your dreams for your child?

   › What are your worries?

   › What are some things your child has told you about his or her experiences at the program?

2. Let us know what times would work for you if none of the options we suggest are good times.

3. Arrive at the scheduled time.

4. Make this adult time. If you will need child care, please let us know.

5. Listen first. While listening, try to focus on what we are saying instead of thinking of answers or questions you want to ask. (We will do the same when listening to you.)

6. Listen then ask questions, voice concerns, share your ideas, and so on.

7. Ask your most pressing question first.

8. Continue your partnership with us. Keep working together to support your child's development and learning.

Families and Educators Together: Building Great Relationships that Support Young Children, by Derry Koralek, Karen Nemeth, and Kelly Ramsey. Copyright © 2019 by the National Association for the Education of Young Children. All rights reserved.

Adapted from H. Seplocha, "Partnerships for Learning: Conferencing with Families," *Young Children* 59 (5): 96–99 (Washington, DC: NAEYC, 2004).

Five

Connecting Home and Program Teaching and Learning

Young children are learning wherever they are—at home, in your setting, and in the community. As a teacher, part of your job is to connect the learning that happens at home with the learning that happens in your program. This will enhance and expand children's experiences and ensure each child's success now and in the future.

Viewing families as their children's first and primary educators has been an integral part of Head Start since the program was launched in 1965. Subsequent initiatives and expansions and recent updated requirements have continued to stress the importance of providing services for children and their families and encouraging home–program connections. All early childhood settings can benefit from Head Start's many years of experience in making home–program connections. To do this, you can acknowledge the family members' skills, life experiences, and assets, and note the ways in which they can contribute these to foster their child's development and learning. Families build on their child's learning wherever it takes place and inspire their children to gain a love of learning for a lifetime. The Family Engagement page on the Head Start Early Childhood Learning and Knowledge Center (ECLKC) website has more information about making home–program connections.

This chapter defines home–program connections that build on what families already do, describes how families can create a learning environment at home, and discusses the kinds of activities children and families can do with simple materials. It also reviews strategies for supporting dual language learners (DLLs), partnering with families to help children build specific skills, and the importance of families becoming their children's media mentors.

Use Connections to Support Everyone

What does it mean to make a home–program connection? It means that you help families encourage learning at home, and families help you support their child's learning in the program. It means that you have a thoughtful process through which family members can ask questions, talk with you and with specialists, and provide insights about their child's experiences, development, and learning. Such connections build family relationships when you share examples of a child's accomplishments and the strategies you use to encourage development and learning for their child. These connections also promote children's development and learning at home when families repeat and build on routines, activities, and experiences that take place at the program.

While each family has its unique strengths, not all families know what it looks like to encourage a child's learning (Edwards 2016). There are several ways to help families learn effective strategies to foster a young child's development. You could create and then post videos on your classroom or program website depicting adult–child interactions that result in learning. Family activities can include opportunities to visit the classroom and observe teachers talking with children and, importantly, listening to children.

Peer relationships can pair a more confident family with a less confident one, allowing the individuals to each learn from the other.

You might find that videos, such as those from Ready Rosie (www.readyrosie.com), have useful suggestions for families. This company offers videos in English and Spanish and provides examples for hundreds of parenting practices and learning interactions between families and their children birth through third grade. Learn more about this series of brief videos in the Appendix on page 122. Another useful resource is the Community and Family Toolkit available on the website of TESOL (www.tesol.org), an organization dedicated to English language teaching. One example is the "family mentors" program, through which more experienced or confident families are invited to connect with a newcomer family. The mentor families receive training and incentives to show appreciation for their work. The TESOL toolkit provides sample handouts, letters, and strategies for successfully conducting this program. Additional organizations that provide resources include

> Head Start provides *The Importance of Home Language* series in 6 languages in addition to English. https://eclkc.ohs.acf.hhs.gov/culture-language/article/importance-home -language-series

> Reading Rockets offers monthly tips for parents in their Growing Readers newsletter. www.readingrockets.org/newsletters/extras

> Zero to Three posts blogs and provides a newsletter for parents of infants and toddlers. www.zerotothree.org/resources/series/parent-favorites

> Teaching at the Beginning has a collection of videos posted to their YouTube channel, which features children learning at home and at school. This is a great example showing a child who worked on a project at school, then brought it home to discuss it with his mother. www.youtube.com/watch?v=q9mIkyfaT-g

Home–program connections are part of an ongoing, circular process through which each partner shares and then uses relevant information to encourage children's development and learning. The process begins at enrollment and continues as long as the child and family are part of the classroom and program community.

Build on What Families Already Do

Part of the enrollment process, initial home visit, and/or first conversations with families include opportunities to find out what families already do to further their children's learning. This will help you avoid "telling" families how to do things they already do. When you have an understanding of a family's current practices, it is easier to build on them. In the following example, Ms. Emery, an infant teacher, wants to learn about the O'Mara family's approach to feeding baby Roxie.

Parents Are Wonderful (PAW): Harnessing Families to Support Literacy Learning

Monica Warren is the director of early learning for Crisp County Schools in Cordele, GA, which operates a pre-K program for 250 children and families in 12 Georgia Lottery-funded pre-K classes. It is also the home base for the preschool special needs program.

CHALLENGE

The literacy assessment scores of young children attending Crisp County schools were below what is typical for their age and grade.

STRATEGY

We initiated a family engagement approach to enhance children's literacy learning through home-based activities. Parents Are Wonderful (PAW) has three parts. Each week a Mobile Literacy Center—in essence a library on wheels—brings books, resources, and family workshops to child care programs, Mothers' Morning Out groups, and community-based parent group meetings in different neighborhoods. PAW also offers school-time family engagement activities and the opportunity for families to earn a Parent Advocate Certificate. Certified advocates help run the Mobile Literacy Center and recruit other families and volunteers.

RESULTS

Children's literacy learning has improved, as evidenced by rising scores on formal assessments. Family participation, which was limited at first, increased during the year as we established a regular schedule for meetings and provided transportation. By surveying families, we learned that a regularly scheduled morning meeting was the most convenient because children were in school or at child development programs. Also, working families could schedule time off once a month in advance, and it was easier for them to work out ride sharing. PAW time is now held the second Friday of each month at 9:00 a.m. and is attended by over two-thirds of the families.

During each PAW time meeting, adults learn a new literacy and social-emotional strategy. They then transition to the classroom where teachers model an activity using the strategies families just learned. Families then practice with their children while the teachers continue to model and offer support. Families appreciate learning something teachers do daily that they can do at home to reinforce learning. Although at first families didn't know what to do, they were eager to do something to improve their children's literacy skills. Families often asked whether PAW would continue after their children moved on to kindergarten.

UPDATE

PAW time is now fully operational 12 months a year, and community partners—such as the housing authority—are supporting efforts to spread PAW time into neighborhoods and communities. PAW time is now offered in kindergarten four times a year. Participation is still high, and families are eager to learn new strategies to support their child's learning.

Ms. Emery: We've noticed that Roxie likes to look around the room when she drinks her bottle. I wonder what she does when you feed her at home.

Mrs. O'Mara: Oh, yes, she does that with us too. Sometimes it takes her a long time to finish nursing.

Ms. Emery: I know what you mean. At this age, babies' vision is improving and they love to look around and learn what's in their environment. We let Roxie take her time.

Mrs. O'Mara: That's good to know. We thought we should hurry her along to make sure she gets the nutrition she needs. But looking and learning are important too. We'll be more patient.

Ms. Emery: Sounds like a good plan for at home and at the program.

Without directly telling Mrs. O'Mara what to do to support Roxie's development, Ms. Emery suggested letting Roxie set the pace for nursing so she could look and learn. And she confirmed that this home–program connection would allow Rosie to learn at home and at the program.

Starting with the phrase "I wonder . . ." is usually a good way to start a conversation with a family member. It has a more inclusive tone than asking, "Do you . . . ?" And it works in various situations. For example, a teacher says to a dad, "I *wonder* why Mateo is having trouble falling asleep at nap time." Her goal is to engage the family as equal partners. She is inviting this father to join her in the wondering, hoping his insights can help to solve the problem so Mateo can take full advantage of nap time. Mateo's dad responds, "Hmm. We've noticed the same thing at bedtime ever since Mateo's sister was born. Perhaps that has something to do with it. We can try giving him some special, big brother attention at bedtime. I'll let you know how it works." In this example, the teacher shared information and the parent suggested a cause and a solution. The stage is set for a follow-up conversation after the family tries the new strategy.

Suggest Developmentally Appropriate Practices

Most, if not all, families are eager to foster their child's development and learning. Some might be so concerned about their child achieving milestones that they want to do more than might be helpful. To help families feel more relaxed about their roles, you might encourage them to observe and pay attention to their children's experiences and emerging skills. Invite them to share what they see and hear with you and jointly express enthusiasm. At a later time—don't take away from this moment—suggest developmentally appropriate ways to build on the child's learning. For example, Charla's grandma is very excited to report that her 3-year-old granddaughter can count to 10 and shares this news with the teacher. She says, "I'm going to teach her to write her numbers now and soon she can do addition." The teacher says, "That's wonderful. Charla has a good memory." She does not say that Charla is still learning to hold a crayon to make scribbles, so she is not ready for writing numbers. Nor does she point out that there are several steps between saying the names for numbers and understanding what they mean and how to use them. Instead, the teacher notes this accomplishment in Charla's folder. In a few days, she will suggest ways to help Charla build on the new skill she learned at home such as by reading number books, counting the strawberries on her plate, and using playdough to build the fine motor skills she will later use for writing numbers. By responding in this way, the teacher is supporting the family as a reciprocal partner rather than behaving as if she knows all the answers.

Book Bags Extend Literacy Learning
from Family Child Care to Home

Stephanie Geneseo is the owner of All Nestled Inn Family Child Care in Chesapeake, OH, which serves six children from birth through age 4 and their families.

CHALLENGE
Some families are eager to support their child's literacy learning but need more information on what is appropriate for children of a certain age. My strong relationships with families allow me to offer suggestions in a friendly and supportive way. Families are busy, however, so I wanted to create an activity that was engaging, easy to implement at home, and beneficial for children.

STRATEGY
Family engagement activities are a key part of my program. One activity that works well is the BABEE (Building a Better Engagement Through Early Childhood Education) bag that is designed to extend daily book experiences from the program setting to each child's home.

Once a month, families receive a BABEE bag related to topics the children have been exploring in the program. Each bag has two age-appropriate books, a manipulatives activity (one we've already introduced), and a guide with simple instructions for using the resources. Also included is a summary questionnaire to document family participation and feedback. Each BABEE bag includes three questions for families. Typical questions include

> What questions did your child ask you about the story?

> What did you notice that your child liked about the book? Disliked?

> Which resources did your child play with after the book was read?

RESULTS
Children and families were excited to use the BABEE bags. Many of the older children can recognize some sight words and enjoy retelling simple stories while paging through books. The families like how the bag is quick, easy, and organized. Because the bags don't have to be returned, the children experience a sense of ownership.

UPDATE
I continue to welcome families' input in designing new BABEE bags. I see myself as communicating to families how much children love books and literacy-related play.

Share Suggested Home Practices with Families

Many families want to know more about child development and supportive strategies they can try at home. This kind of information is most useful when delivered in a variety of formats and in small doses over time. Create family-focused handouts, emails, short videos, or whatever else works for the children's families. Be sure to include examples that match the families' interests, skills, language, and culture. For example, when sharing ideas with parents of toddlers, you might include examples related to learning self-help skills such as hand-washing and dressing. Listen to their responses so you can adjust your recommendations to respect the family's cultural traditions.

The Touchpoints Approach

Renowned pediatrician and author T. Berry Brazelton transformed the understanding of parents navigating the "touchpoints" of a child's development. *Touchpoints* are the pivotal times when a child experiences a milestone, such as learning to walk. Mastering milestones creates uncertainty—Brazelton calls this *disequilibrium*—for children as they prepare themselves for the growth to come. These touchpoints can be challenging for parents, and they may be times when families reach out to educators for guidance.

Here is an example of a teacher and family partnering while a child is experiencing a touchpoint.

Twelve-month-old Wiley is learning to walk. She devotes all her energy to practicing this new skill. These energy bursts cause Wiley to regress in other areas. Instead of following her usual pattern of sleeping through the night, she now wakes up and cries for a few minutes. Formerly an eager eater, Wiley now rejects food she once enjoyed. The touchpoint—learning to walk—is a sign of Wiley's progress. At home and at the program, she has had opportunities to pull herself up and engage in other precursors to walking. Wiley's parents might see this milestone as a sign their baby is growing up too fast, miss the days of infancy, and have some fears about what it means to parent a toddler.

As a true partner, Wiley's teacher supports the child's family members by discussing the milestone and what changes it will bring. She is sensitive to the ways in which one event, in this case learning to walk, can have many interpretations. The parents are probably excited, but also concerned about what they will need to do in response to their child's new skill—making sure the home environment is safe for a new walker, for example. The Touchpoints approach provides a framework for both the parent and the teacher to hold assumptions about the child's new behavior. This milestone itself can serve as a provocation to link the child's new learning with developmentally appropriate learning experiences to offer at home. These might mirror practices used in the classroom—for example, arranging sturdy pieces of furniture so Wiley can walk safely between them. Or her teacher might talk about typical classroom interactions and changes to the environment that families can use to support Wiley. Her dad remarks, "Wow! Now she'll be able to reach things on the coffee table. We'll have to be careful about what we leave there."

Create a Safe Place for Play

The home is where everyone in the family lives, works, and plays together. Most learning takes place at home—it's where children spend the most time. Children need a dedicated area where they can read, write, play, and so on, alone and with others. When children feel comfortable and free to try new things, they develop and learn. Their "area" could be a bottom drawer or shelf in a kitchen cabinet, a small table and chair or a booster or high chair at the kitchen table, or baskets of books and toys in a corner. When families display children's work and photos of them playing and learning, children learn, "I can do many wonderful things."

Children can thrive and learn while playing with toys that match their interests and abilities and that offer opportunities to use them creatively. These toys can be new items or well-loved second-hand toys. What they need most is a safe and happy home where they can learn who they are and what they can do. There are low-cost play materials that families can make for children to use at home.

Suggest Basic Materials

Most families with young children are busy people and may think they do not have the time to focus on learning at home. But you can help them see that simply spending time with their children and talking with them, making best use of their time together, and providing a safe place for exploration and learning contributes greatly to the child's success.

You might suggest that families have a few of the following fascinating materials.

For infants

> Soft balls to throw and crawl to

> Pots and pans and spoons to bang them with

> Sturdy plastic cups and dishes to explore and begin pretending

> Clean, empty food containers to bang together

> Small pieces of fabric to touch

> Dolls, stuffed animals, and simple props such as blankets and bottles to begin imitating the care they are experiencing

> Board books and cloth books

> Paper bags, magazines, and advertising flyers to crumple or tear

For toddlers

Any of the above items that are still of interest and

> Ribbons, scarves, and large fabric pieces to dance with

> Doll stroller or carriage to push when learning to walk

> Sock puppets to "talk" with

> Large washable, nontoxic markers and crayons and large pieces of paper for scribbling

> Cars, trucks, and other vehicles to push along the floor

> Cardboard boxes to crawl into and out of

> Nontoxic glue and tape for simple projects

> Recycled containers and large bottle caps for filling and dumping

> Child-safe photo albums with pictures of family members, pets, and home

For preschoolers

Any of the above items that are still of interest and

> Crayons, markers, and paper for writing and drawing
> Construction paper
> Book binding items such as a stapler, hole punch, and laces
> Recycled paper and fabric and yarn scraps for creations
> Hats and other clothing for dress-up play
> Natural materials such as pinecones, leaves, and acorns or whatever is found in your area
> Buttons, keys, shells, and other items to sort and categorize
> Picture books

An early childhood program might provide several of the items from the lists above in a welcome packet at the start of the year. Ask local businesses for donations of backpacks or tote bags and items to include in them. Also share found and recycled items to convey the message, "You have many things at home that make great play materials." Include suggestions, illustrated with photos, for how children and families might use the materials. Be sure to provide written suggestions in families' home languages and in English.

Encourage Reading Aloud Every Day

For years, educational researchers and teachers have pointed to the benefits of reading aloud with young children. The experience of reading with a loving family member—in the child's home language or in English—is a wonderful bonding and learning experience. The experience of turning pages, looking at pictures, and listening to a story help to teach children about how books work—something that will help them build early literacy skills. And the book's content allows children to understand new information, vocabulary, feelings, and problem solving through the characters' experiences. Reading aloud every day is one of the best ways to support home–program connections. Through reading, families can introduce and talk about new words, encourage early literacy skills and knowledge, highlight special interests, and build connections with their child that lead to strong and lasting relationships. In addition, books provide something to talk about beyond the here and now. Some parents are not confident about or experienced in reading aloud to their children. You can help by sharing brief video clips or hosting demonstrations or classes to give families some ideas about reading and talking about books with their children.

Reading aloud is a major indicator of a child's later success in school and in life. It's important to understand that not all family members can read, know how to read aloud with children, remember being read to when they were young, or have the time and energy needed to read with their children. Instead, it might be more helpful to show families how to make reading aloud part of their daily life.

You might also suggest specific activities families can do in addition to reading, such as

> Tell stories—true ones about yourself and others. "When my dog Ben was a puppy, he . . ."

> Post or share a list of things to do after turning off devices.
  "Do a puzzle, go for a walk, play catch."

> Post or share a list of things to do together with devices. "Take and send photos to relatives, play games, look at insect videos."

> Post or share a list of things to do with what you have on hand. "Make soup, draw on the sidewalk with chalk, cut pictures out of old magazines."

> Think of everyone in a child's home as teachers. "Diego is 10 now. If he teaches Gabriela to play checkers, they can play together."

Recommend Everyday Actions as Opportunities to Learn

It's important for families to understand that many of the everyday routines and activities at home can be opportunities to foster their child's development and learning. Just as teachers plan ways to include children in classroom and program routines, so too can families involve children during the day's events.

The things families do every day at home—cooking, cleaning, bathing, diapering, and so on—can all be times when a child is involved and learning. In most homes, routines take up much of the day, so it's wise to do them with children. Young children can set and clear the table, feed pets, fold laundry, tidy rooms, and hold, pass, and learn to use tools. By taking part in routines, children learn to follow instructions, predict what might happen next, feel safe and secure, and feel proud to be contributing to home life. Even babies can take part from an early age—holding a clean diaper, pulling off socks, lifting a bottom, and so on. Children at any age can benefit when adults fill those daily routines with lots of talking.

Here are some additional strategies you can share with families to encourage daily interactions with their children at home:

> Talk together, anywhere and everywhere, and about almost anything. Talking builds relationships, introduces vocabulary, and builds on a child's interests and experiences. "The water has emptied out of the tub. Now it's time to put the toys away. Say 'good-bye piggy,' 'good-bye boat,' 'good-bye duck.'"

> Listen and respond to children's communications, including coos, gurgles, words, and sentences. This practice is called *serve and return*. When you look at and respond to the child's vocalizations and language, you help build the brain connections that support the child's development of both communication and social skills. For example, a grandfather sees granddaughter Jerri wiggling happily in her high chair. He bends to her level, looks her in the eyes, and says, "I saw you smiling when I came in the kitchen. Are you happy to see me? I'm happy to see you!" Jerri lifts her arms, saying, "Up! Up!"

> Explain actions in real time. Describe for your child what you are doing while you are doing it. "Uh-oh. These clothes don't fit in this laundry bag. The bag is too small. We need a bigger bag. Or we could try two bags."

> Model how to do something. Instead of just saying, "Don't put too much toothpaste on the brush," teach by doing. "Watch me give a gentle squeeze so just enough toothpaste comes out. Now you try it."

> Show respect because children learn to be respectful when people treat them with respect. To show respect, crouch at a child's level, speak softly, avoid yelling, and respond when your child seeks attention, even if it's to say, "I'll be there in a minute."

> Ask open-ended questions that have more than one right answer. They usually result in conversations because they can't be answered with just one word. For example, when you ask, "What things did you do today during outdoor play?" your child is likely to offer information you can use to continue the discussion. "That sounds like fun. What do you think you and Max will build tomorrow?"

> Wonder together. Explore inside and outside and learn about the world. "I wonder what will happen if we eat our soup with a fork. I wonder what we could use to make our sandwiches today. I wonder what's under your blanket. I wonder where that squirrel is going." Parents and children can also wonder about solutions to problems like "I can't find your mittens. I wonder what we can put on your hands to keep warm. Maybe socks would work for today."

> Use effective praise that tells your child you notice her efforts and accomplishments. Describe what you saw her do and what happened as a result. "I noticed you put the beads on a tray before you started threading them. They stayed in place and didn't roll on the floor. You used a lot of colors in your necklace."

> Teach a new skill by breaking it down into small steps so your child can accomplish each one. For example, learning to fasten shoes starts with learning to put them on. Next might come fastening Velcro straps. And then, when he moves to wearing shoes with laces, help him learn to tie them.

> Work as a team to accomplish a task. A lot of learning takes place when adults and children work together. "You can hold the dustpan while I use the broom to sweep into it."

> Offer a few simple choices. Life is filled with opportunities to make choices; children can practice when offered a few simple options. For example, "We're making pancakes today. Would you like to add blueberries or strawberries or both?" Allowing children to make choices teaches them to decide which one is best for the situation.

Learning Stories

Learning stories are a form of observation and documentation that is written in a narrative format. They are positive and written to the child. Teachers provide details on how a child engages with materials, interacts with others, uses toys and materials, and experiences routines and activities at the program. When writing the learning story, the teacher leaves space for input and exchange from the family. They are another way to support home–program connections.

Here is an example of how a learning story can emerge and evolve:

Terrence and the Cowboy Hat

Terrence, age 4, brightens when his teacher, Mr. Hernandez, says the class will be studying hats. When Mr. Hernandez places a cowboy hat in the middle of the circle at group time, Terrence gets so excited he can hardly sit still. At pick-up time, Mr. Hernandez tells Terrence's mother, "Terrence is thrilled we will be studying hats." His mother says, "Oh, yes. Terrence's dad is a cowboy. He's been riding horses since he was 2." Terrence smiles and says, "My daddy is going to ride in the rodeo this year." Mr. Hernandez smiles too.

The story can emerge and evolve.

Mr. Hernandez asks Terrence's mother to tell him more about her son's interest in cowboy hats. He wants to add it to the story. She says, "At home, we have scrapbooks from all the years Terrence's dad has been riding horses and competing in rodeos. I'll bring them in to share with everyone!"

This example shows the richness that can result from engaging families in writing learning stories. Thinking of this story, what learning stories could you capture in your classroom? In what concrete ways are you connecting with parents and families to extend the learning environment at school?

Learn more about learning stories in a teacher's blog (https://tomdrummond.com /looking-closely-at-children /writing-learning-stories) and in a *Teaching Young Children* article (NAEYC.org/resources /pubs/tyc/dec2016/learning -stories).

> Step out of the action to observe. Sometimes parenting, and learning at home, is about taking time to watch, listen, and learn as a child plays alone or with family members and friends. The observer is likely to identify the skills a child has mastered along with ones he or she is still working on. Observations can identify interests or skills such as when a child talks about her day to her stuffed animals. Families can jot down or record notes in a memory notebook or journal (print or digital) about what their child does and says, and how he or she responds to others. This useful information can guide family conversations and activities and help teachers in planning and in keeping track of a child's progress.

You can think of several ways to share ideas like this with families. A good place to start is to think about how families would like to receive this kind of information. You might post ideas on a bulletin board, or include some tips in an email, newsletter, text, or letter. There are several text messaging services that provide this kind of information to families, such as www.text4baby.org. You could encourage families to sign up for that free service, which is available in Spanish and English.

Provide Activities Families Can Do at Home with Their Children

Early childhood programs often create and send home learning activities as a way for families to follow up on classroom activities or as an opportunity to set the stage for an upcoming experience. Suggestions for these kinds of activities fill the pages of books, blogs, websites, and more. The most appropriate and effective activities require no more than simple materials— provided by the program if not usually available at home—and have specific goals for learning. They include step-by-step instructions and illustrations or photos; they're translated into home languages; and they suggest ways to report to the teacher on what the child did and learned. In addition, it's important to provide opportunities for children to build socioemotional skills, understand concepts, gain knowledge, and build skills in all domains. Luckily, many home and program experiences and play materials involve and reinforce multiple domains at the same time. A few ideas include

> Bedtime Math: www.bedtimemath.org/bedtime-math-for-families

> Let's Play from Zero to Three: available as an app in the iTunes store

> Sesame Street in Communities: www.sesamestreetincommunities.org

> Too Small to Fail: www.toosmall.org

> 20 Fun Indoor Games: www.todaysparent.com/toddler/20-fun-indoor-games

Another way to boost home learning is by creating home learning tote bags or backpacks focused on a specific area of the curriculum. Many programs offer book bags that can be checked out of the classroom library and include a book, related props (e.g., puppets), suggestions for reading and talking about the book, and a way to share feedback with other readers, such as a journal. Teachers can also create bags related to music, movement, art, math, block building, cooking, nature, and so on. These too can include a journal or other feedback method. Once again, these can build on program activities or introduce something new, and they should include everything needed to make the best use of the contents. For example, if the class is planning a trip to the zoo, the backpack could include nonfiction and fiction books

Including Families in Curriculum Studies

Ana Azcarate is an early childhood special education teacher at President Avenue Elementary School in Harbor City, CA, which is a part of the Los Angeles Unified School District. The school's mission is to provide quality educational programs to develop sensitivity, respect, and high expectations for a diverse population who become independent, lifelong learners. Programs include an extended transitional kindergarten and preschool collaborative classroom (ETK-PCC). This collaborative classroom serves up to 16 children who are typically developing and up to eight children who have disabilities. The staff include a general education teacher, a special education teacher, a special education assistant, and a general education assistant. Families are encouraged to participate in the six-hour preschool program. Most families are young and working, and some are single parents.

CHALLENGE   We were missing opportunities to involve families in children's learning at the beginning, middle, and end of a unit of study. Our previous curriculum didn't easily support family interactions, but our new curriculum underscores the need for and importance of family partnerships by not only facilitating, but also referencing research that supports family engagement.

STRATEGY   At the beginning of each study, we used the curriculum resources (e.g., letters to families provided in their home language) to introduce the topic and let families know how they could participate and support their children's learning. We included tips on how to expand their child's knowledge at home. For example, during our tree study we asked that parents take their children on a "tree walk" to collect tree parts to further investigate the topic. To further enhance learning we also invite family members who might work in gardening or horticulture to come and speak to us about what they do. We asked them to talk about trees, explore trees, play sorting games with tree parts, count tree parts, build a collage, and many other activities.

At the end of the tree study, families came to our celebration. Children sang songs or recited rhymes, presented a play, exhibited artwork, showed their families projects, and together with their family members completed a study-related activity. In the first year, some working family members could not attend the planned activities or celebrations. In our second year, we expanded the use of technology through ClassDojo, a classroom communication app that allows us to connect with families by sharing photos, videos, and messages throughout the day. Families can also send messages or upload pictures to the app.

RESULTS   Partnering with families and counting them as stakeholders in curriculum implementation empowers them to actively foster their child's curiosity about the world. We get positive feedback from families and hear of their excitement after collecting items for studies, creating things with their child, or coming to the end-of-study celebrations. But witnessing the children's enthusiasm when they share about how they sang to their families or collected items over a weekend to donate for the study is always priceless!

UPDATE   In collaboration with two other preschool teachers, we continue to plan ways to involve families and make stronger family connections within our program.

(*Goodnight, Gorilla* would be a good one!), a list of reminders of field trip behaviors, small zoo animal toys to play with, and crayons and paper to keep and use after the visit to document something the child saw or did. Teachers can review the feedback from families who try these activities at home and use what they learn to support individual children, plan curriculum for the whole class, or make changes in the activities to make them more appropriate for home use.

Support Home Languages and Cultures

Every family has a culture—put simply, it's what they think is important (e.g., learning a second language, keeping in touch with old friends, saying grace before meals) and how they do things (e.g., walking instead of driving whenever possible, packing a healthy lunch instead of buying fast food), along with the planned and unplanned actions that are part of what makes the family unique. For example, in one family, reading might be a practice that is passed down from adults to children, or home cooking might be an important part of a family's daily mealtimes. A family culture can include how you carry out daily routines as well as how you celebrate special events and holidays. In one family, everyone gets new underwear for special days—first day of school, taking the SATs, going on a job interview, and so on. It's just a practice they hope will bring good luck.

Children learn about their family's culture from the valuable conversations and stories they engage in at home. This is an important foundation for their development and future learning. Families may feel pressured to imitate the school learning experience with "educational" toys and activities for their child, but you want them to understand that you value the ways they pass down family traditions and ways of life to their children as well.

Another important role families play is to support their child's continued learning in the home language. You can assure families that giving their child a good foundation of learning in the rich vocabulary they use at home actually helps with later learning at school and in English. Research shows that high-quality home language is important, and growing up bilingual is an advantage for children. You can find handouts for families to support these activities that are available in several languages: *The Importance of Home Language* series (https://eclkc.ohs.acf. hhs.gov/culture-language/article/importance-home-language-series) and Reading Tip Sheets for Parents (www.colorincolorado.org/reading-tip-sheets-parents).

Partner with Families to Build Needed Skills

Sometimes a child needs to work on a particular skill—perhaps she is having difficulty drawing and writing and needs to build her fine motor skills. Showing families how to support this skill with fun activities at home will help to keep them informed about their child's progress, while balancing out the times that the child is exposed to that practice. You can help families be successful by giving them easy-to-do ideas. To reinforce a math skill, their child can count the items being purchased at the grocery store. To practice a physical skill, their child can jump over sticks in the park. For young children who receive physical, speech, or occupational therapy, therapists generally work with the family and the program staff. To provide the most effective support for this kind of skill development, there should be a consistent approach at home and in the program. Home–program connections are stepping stones that can facilitate significant progress in the development of needed skills that further children's growth and learning.

Book Parties: Celebrating Books Together

Dawn Brown directs the Christ the King Early Education Center in Topeka, KS, which serves 210 children from infancy through school age. Their mission is "to provide a warm, safe, and caring environment while teaching early development skills based on a sound family partnership."

CHALLENGE
Despite a mission that specifically cited the importance of family partnerships, there was a need for families to become more involved in the center as well as in their children's lives.

STRATEGY
Four times a year, we hold book parties at pick-up times from 5 to 6 p.m. For each party, we focus on a different author—like Eric Litwin (*Pete the Cat*) or Laura Numeroff (*If You Give a Moose a Muffin*)—or illustrator like Jerry Pinkney, Ashley Bryan, and others. The parties are times when teachers can connect with families to share their children's efforts and progress. Our planning process involves community organizations so families can learn about the local activities and services that are available. For example, the local zoo helped with a Curious George party. To support children's learning, we plan adult–child activities that focus on math, science, art, nutrition, and fine motor, gross motor, and social skills.

RESULTS
The book parties have helped families to discover interesting new ways to connect with their children through books and activities. The book event planning process allows teachers to spend quality time working as a team. We enhance the events by using our community's resources, such as our local resource and referral, YMCA, farmers' market, computer buddies, and Interactive Metronome (a therapeutic modality that focuses on cognitive and motor skills).

UPDATE
We continue to hold book parties and have added opportunities for children and families to play different games, such as Go Fish, Uno, and Candyland.

Prepare Families to Be Their Child's Media Mentor

Technology and digital media have a growing place in our society and in the lives of many families. Early childhood educators can't tell families what to do, but they can serve as mentors to model appropriate technology use by and around young children. When sharing information about the importance of having conversations about technology with young children, you might also mention research showing that when adults use devices, it may reduce the time available for valuable interactions they could be having with children (Christakis 2018). Also consider providing information for families about internet safety and about developmentally appropriate activities using technology. Find more information in *Family Engagement in the Digital Age* (Donohue 2016). Thoughtful sharing of resources and advice can help family members become valuable media mentors and guide their children's digital learning. In addition, the American Academy of Pediatrics published children and media tips in 2018 (www.aap.org/en-us/about-the-aap/aap-press-room/news-features-and-safety-tips/Pages/Children-and-Media-Tips.aspx) and the Common Sense Media website has an entire section on "Advice for Parents" with articles searchable by the age of the child or by topics (www.commonsensemedia.org/screen-time).

There are many ways for teachers to use home–program connections to enhance children's learning in both settings. This chapter describes ideas and possibilities that can make a difference in the impact of your work and in the outcomes for children. When families enroll a child in an early childhood setting, they have already been fostering their child's learning since birth. Now they will continue their journey in partnership with you and your colleagues. What family members learn about supporting their child's learning at home and at the program will set the stage for continued engagement as their child progresses through the school years.

Reflection Questions

Now that you have read this chapter, consider the following questions:

1. What do you do to ensure all families see themselves as their child's primary educator? How do you build on their cultural, family, and personal assets?

2. Imagine you are meeting a family for the first time. What do you want to learn about them? What do you want them to learn about you? How will you communicate that working together as a team is best for their child?

3. How can you start writing learning stories with input from families? What do you think you and the families will gain from these stories? How will they support the child and the child–parent relationship?

Partnering with the Community

Every community has different assets, needs, interests, and resources for families and children. Your program is one of those assets, but the services you offer can be enhanced through partnerships with community groups.

There are three significant ways teachers can ensure that community partnerships are beneficial:

1. Learn about community organizations and services and share that information with families who need them.

2. Invite local groups to contribute materials, volunteers, and other resources for children and families.

3. Collaborate with community organizations to advocate for children, families, and the program.

You can get involved in local activities, join committees, and build community awareness about the importance of early childhood education to meet the needs of all kinds of children and families. For example, you might participate in a health fair committee to learn what other participants offer and to be the voice of preschool teachers in the planning. Most agencies are eager to find new ways to support children and families, so it is likely that your overtures will be met with positive responses.

This chapter describes ways to develop partnerships with your counterparts in community agencies. Such partnerships benefit children, families, teachers, and your community organization partners.

Build Relationships with Elementary Schools

One of the most critical groups to partner with is the elementary schools that children will attend. Preschool teachers play an important role in encouraging families to be advocates for their children as they get ready to enter kindergarten. This is especially important for families who must make decisions about which school will be the best placement for their children. When children have birthdays that are close to the school district's kindergarten entry cutoff date, families may need to consider whether the time is right for their child to start kindergarten. Decisions such as this are based on the characteristics of individual children and the expectations of the elementary school. For some children it might be appropriate to spend more time in preschool before enrolling in kindergarten. Families depend on teachers to be knowledgeable about state and district rules, and about research that can help the family make decisions. For children who may need an individualized education plan (IEP) due to a developmental delay or a diagnosed disability, families could be learning for the first time about their rights to participate in creating that plan and influencing decisions about assessments, evaluations, and services for their children. This can be an overwhelming responsibility for families, and teachers who have accurate information about the options and about family rights will be very helpful throughout the decision-making part of this transition. In fact, many knowledgeable preschool teachers accompany families to IEP planning meetings at the school to provide support as families develop confidence and knowledge.

Families of children who are dual language learners (DLLs) may also need to advocate for their children. As children get ready to transition to kindergarten, they will experience entry assessments and language screenings. In some school districts, officials use the results to determine whether to place the child in a bilingual kindergarten or an English as a second language setting with varying levels of language development services. Schools make these placement decisions, but they send a determination letter to families for their signature. This is another area where a preschool teacher can help families understand the options and their rights and help them decide what they will or will not approve for their child.

Maintain relationships with the local school districts. Participate on committees and in joint professional development offerings. As the family's first advocate, you can be the role model they need to advocate for the rest of their child's school life.

A Teacher's Role in Recruiting Families

As a teacher, you are also a member of the community in which your program is located. You might be called upon to build relationships in the community to let families know what your program offers. Here is an example:

> When I visited my daughter's family in their new home, we took our granddaughter out for an afternoon stroll in the new neighborhood. A few blocks from home, we met two young women carrying clipboards. They were talking with families who had young children to tell them about their child development center, child care program, and playgroup activities. Most centers wait for families to find them, but these teachers and staff went out into the neighborhood to meet the families as they walked to the store, waited at the bus stop, or headed to the playground. They handed out flyers to interested families and took their phone numbers and email addresses so they could follow up later.

For further information on *moving on to kindergarten:*

Learn about the Boston Children's Museum's ongoing exhibit—a model kindergarten classroom that introduces children and adults to what a typical kindergarten is like. The classroom includes learning centers such as a reading and writing corner and is staffed with "teachers" who can answer questions about the nuts and bolts of the kindergarten experience. www .bostonchildrensmuseum.org /exhibits-programs/exhibits /countdown-kindergarten

The museum has also created a Let's Get Ready for Kindergarten! kit for preschool teachers to help them create learning opportunities, based on the Massachusetts Early Learning Standards that help children get ready for their new schools. Using the materials in the kit, teachers can create a "Let's play school" setting in their classroom. Find the guidebook and activities at http://school-readiness.org/countdown -kindergarten.

ReadySteps: Playgroups for Families and Children

Shannon C. M. Banks is the community education program manager for the ReadySteps Program, a part of ReadyKids, Inc., a 95-year old private nonprofit organization. ReadyKids, Inc. is dedicated to ensuring that every young child in Charlottesville, VA, is ready to learn, ready for relationships, and ultimately ready for life!

CHALLENGE
In several communities in the area served by ReadyKids, Inc., many families and young children do not have access to early education, leading to limited opportunities for adults and children to interact with others so they are ready for kindergarten.

STRATEGY
ReadyKids, Inc., wanted to help families strengthen their children's readiness for school. ReadySteps was created as a free family-focused early education program in designated neighborhoods. Two ReadySteps vans with two staff and an array of developmentally appropriate toys and education materials travel to different community centers across town. There are eight playgroup sessions per week, each lasting two hours. Children ages birth to 5 years and their families are eligible to enroll, and each site enrolls between 10 and 50 children and caregivers. Playgroups are led by educators who engage children in learning experiences that promote interactions and encourage development of self-regulation skills. Family members and caregivers participate with their children and, through observations, learn about child growth and development.

RESULTS
I saw signs that the program was successful when current participants began encouraging other families and friends to come to playgroups. Many brought new families to their first group and introduced them to other playgroup families. Community organizations refer clients to the ReadySteps program, request to be partners, and ask for resources and support for families. Families form bonds and friendships within and across languages and cultures. The program has become a recognized and valued community partner in working with families to prepare their children for success.

UPDATE
The program continues to grow through partnerships with elementary schools and community agencies. Of the children who attended at least 10 playgroups, more than 80 percent achieved developmentally appropriate school readiness skills, and every child demonstrated positive parent–child interactions.

Collaborate with Community Groups

Many families of young children are not aware of the numerous recreational and supportive services that are available within their own communities. They may pass libraries, swimming pools, parks, and so on, but not know how to learn about or access these family-friendly services. Teachers can provide this information so all families can benefit from the resources in their community. The fourth principle of family engagement states: "Programs use learning activities at home and in the community to enhance each child's early learning and encourage families' efforts to create a learning environment beyond the program" (NAEYC, n.d.).

Collaborating with community organizations helps to build awareness of what is available in the neighborhood and beyond. You might

> Partner with a farmers' market to bring fresh foods to the program or provide seeds for families to start a home garden

> Coordinate with a local bakery to bring loaves of challah to the center every Friday for families to purchase on their way home

> Work with a bank or credit union to offer financial literacy classes to help families learn about checking and savings accounts, how to secure funding for a home down payment, sources of micro-loans, or how to start a small home-based business

> Invite someone from the parks department to come in and show children and families about the features and free programs they offer to the community

> Help the local food pantry establish an annex on-site, open monthly so families can select healthy foods to prepare at home

Learning activities are not limited to the home and may occur at many places in the community, such as in libraries, museums, and family resource centers (Van Voorhis et al. 2013, 4). Businesses may also support learning as when a laundromat or barber shop provides a basket of children's books. A school district in rural New Jersey hosts a family carnival every year called Under the Big Top. Like many carnivals, there are games, food, music, and activities. What makes this event unique is that the local police department runs the face painting booth, the speech and hearing service runs the ring toss, and the public library runs the snack table and brings library card applications for all the families. This event is a fun opportunity to build connections to the early childhood community, and it gives children and families a chance to interact with local service providers in a relaxed atmosphere.

Another valuable community partnership is between early childhood programs and health service providers. Health clinic staff, nutritionists, and dentists may visit programs to do health screenings or provide health education for children and families. Universities may send audiology students to perform free hearing screenings. This also helps families learn more about the health services available in the community.

To learn more about *accessing health services in the community:*

Read *Raising Young Children in a New Country: Supporting Early Learning and Healthy Development* (available in four languages) on the ECLKC website (https:// eclkc.ohs.acf.hhs.gov).

Assess Current and Future Partnerships

Which groups does your program partner with now? What new partnerships could be established to meet families' needs and interests? How can you find out what kinds of collaborations and partnerships are of interest and use to families? Remember: whenever you partner with other organizations and professionals, you are likely to be as valuable to them as they are to you. After all, you are an expert in early childhood education.

The options for community partnerships vary from place to place. Some may be familiar to you and some may surprise you. Several experts have written about the importance of community contributions that allow children to become engaged in and supported by their community as a way to prevent isolation, cultural misunderstandings, and bias (Children's Bureau, n.d.; Derman-Sparks, LeeKeenan, & Nimmo 2015). This list of potential partners includes suggestions for collaborative activities that might inspire your own creative ideas for community involvement.

> Police departments (provide car seat installation guidance)

> Transportation (help families find locally funded transport to healthcare and other appointments)

> Housing (explain subsidy programs, rentals, and legal issues such as signing leases)

> Food (Women, Infants, and Children [WIC] and food pantries provide free food and share recipes for low-cost, nutritious meals)

> Cultural activities (invite participation in and attendance at fairs, sales, celebrations, and performances)

> Counseling (link families with appropriate services for children and adults)

> Recreation (provide information on classes, parks, and open gyms for adults and children)

> Literacy supports (provide classes at the program)

> Child care resource and referral (distribute information about parenting, child care subsidies, and other resources that help families)

> Social organizations (help families connect with each other and develop their own networks)

> Senior centers (invite seniors to volunteer at the program)

> Early intervention (offer informational sessions for families and bring services in to early childhood programs as needed)

> Public and private schools (collaborate with early childhood programs to welcome and involve families in the community and pave the way for children's transitions)

> Summer camps (provide a variety of options for additional care and family activities)

> After school and enrichment activities (offer fun learning activities such as crafts, sports, languages, performing arts, STEM activities, and nature exploration)

> Community service organizations (Kiwanis, chamber of commerce, and other associations conduct fundraisers to meet the needs of families and local early childhood programs)

> Funders and foundations (provide funding for a family field trip or a family literacy take-home library)

> Affiliates or chapters of professional associations like NAEYC, NAFCC, NHSA, NNELL (connect teachers and administrators with other professionals to share ideas for family engagement activities, resources, and funding)

> Colleges/universities (conduct site visits, serve as student teachers, and lead workshops)

> Legal services (answer questions about immigration and citizenship requirements)

> Thrift shops (offer discounts on certain days for program teachers and families)

> Museums, zoos, and aquariums (museum educators may visit early childhood programs or offer special family access and activities)

The Family and Community Engagement Framework of Head Start's National Center on Parent, Family, and Community Engagement has more information about community partnerships.

Establish New Partnerships

Partnerships with community agencies allow your program to expand the resources available to families. These partnerships require planning and nurturing and, like many things in early childhood, they rely on reciprocal relationships.

To get started, create a list of community agencies that serve the families of your community, particularly families with young children. Ask families about their interests and needs during enrollment and at other times during the year. Canvass the neighborhood, ask colleagues, and consult with administrators to identify available services.

A next step is to contact local organizations and introduce yourself and your program. Look on the organization's website to identify the name and role carried out by a potential partner. While on the website, learn what they offer and how families can take part. If possible, stop by to share a brochure about your program. Ask if the contact is available. If not, leave your card and an invitation for this person to contact you. You might also introduce yourself and your program through email.

Follow up as needed to talk with the contact. Invite him or her to tour the program and learn about the children, families, and staff. During the visit, inquire about the organization's mission, the services they offer, and how families can access them. Be sure to exchange ideas about how the two entities can contribute to and enhance each other's work.

Once you have identified partners, invite them to take part in initiatives planned by your program. For example, if you are planning a family carnival you might need prizes; for a family gardening event, you will need pots, tools, and plants. Think creatively about which groups and individuals could be possible partners and sponsors. For example, could the local dollar store provide prizes? Could YMCA coaches help plan and run games? Could the neighborhood hardware store provide gardening supplies?

An Early Childhood Program Sends Families Home with Veggies

We uncovered opportunities to support relationship building with and between families. As parents recognized the significance of the children's efforts, care, and thought in the garden, they were happily dragged along the rows by their children to pick vegetables and herbs for mealtime at home. Families, including older siblings, attend the center's annual Harvest Festival in droves, having the opportunity to taste-test salsa, pickles, and other goodies grown and created by the children for this celebration of community.

(Nimmo & Hallett 2008, 35)

Does the botanical garden have a volunteer who could offer gardening tips?

When asking for assistance, be sure to state your goals clearly and ask for what you need to achieve them. Try to connect your organization's goals with those of the partner. Explain how the contribution will support families, your program, and the partner's program.

Once you have established a relationship with another organization, it's important to actively keep it going. Stay in touch with your contacts at various community groups. Let them know how children and families are benefiting from their services and participation.

Remember to ask what you can do for your partners. For example, you can provide expert advice on what children and families need, their interests, their time commitments, and so on. And you can support their family engagement efforts.

Be sure to acknowledge your partners in print and digital materials about the program. Explain what they do and how it enhances the lives of children and families.

Foster Strong Relationships with Libraries

Public libraries, found in almost every US community, are natural partners in addressing the interests and needs of young children and families. When libraries and early childhood programs work together, they can open the world of learning for children and their families. A few examples include the following:

> Local libraries often provide resources in multiple languages for children and families. They offer engaging events, classes, and activities and access to computers and other digital devices. Many early childhood programs help families visit the library and obtain library cards.

> Library outreach programs, such as bookmobiles, often bring literacy resources and services to early childhood programs in hard-to-reach areas. They may have digital stories and activities for families available through their website (Nemeth & Campbell 2013).

> The Philadelphia Public Library recently contracted with Ready Rosie, a company that offers family engagement tools and support, to make free videos available to all families in their area. Schools and child care programs encourage families to enroll in the program. Families receive links to brief videos every week giving them ideas to support their child's learning at home and in the community with reading, writing, math, and science activities.

> The Every Child Ready to Read initiative provides resources and training for children's librarians. Their goal was to change from offering a child-only story time experience to a focus on creating programs and events for children and family members that could model literacy and learning activities for the home (Celano & Neuman 2015).

Many libraries focus on achieving family engagement goals, such as the ones listed below. Consider the following as you determine the best ways to establish linkages with your library to ensure children and families can benefit from their services:

> Libraries reach out to families to promote the programs, collections, and services that are vital in a knowledge economy. *Your program could offer to collect and share what you have learned about the interests and needs of families.*

> Libraries provide guidance on and modeling of specific actions that family members can take to support learning, reaffirming families' important roles and strengthening feelings of efficacy. *Your program can work with the library to make sure all families learn read-aloud tips and strategies that make stories come to life.*

> Libraries offer opportunities for families to build peer-to-peer relationships, social networks, and parent–child relationships. *Once again, you and your counterparts who are library staff can exchange your knowledge and coordinate your practices to achieve this shared goal.*

Libraries are expanding their community partnerships; combining resources and extending their range; improving children and families' well-being; and linking new learning opportunities. Your program is well-placed to become one of the library's partners, working together to meet this goal (Lopez, Caspe, & McWilliams 2016).

Encourage Families to Be Advocates

Some family members enjoy and do well in sharing their views with decision makers. With encouragement and a little direction, they are eager to step up and voice their views on behalf of children beyond your early childhood setting. Engaging families in advocacy work as their children grow and continue in school ensures that families will thrive as lifelong learners. Advocacy on behalf of children and families can take place on various levels, such as local, state, and national. The advocacy efforts can engage both adults and children in the process. For instance, a program might plan and host family events to advocate for funding for early childhood programs in rural areas. Simple letter-writing campaigns to legislators are great ways to involve families in advocating for funding for the community's child care and early education systems. In another example, each year families across the United States celebrate Child Abuse Awareness month in April. They make blue ribbon ties and wear them to remind community members to support children and families. What does your program do to engage families as advocates for young children and families?

Identifying and encouraging families to engage in advocacy supports the fifth principle of family engagement: "Programs invite families to participate in program-level decision and wider advocacy efforts" (NAEYC, n.d.).

Form a Program Diversity Team

One way to enhance a program's sense of community to engage all families is bringing people together with a shared goal of supporting diversity. In many settings this is called a *diversity team* and includes volunteers, staff, family members, and community representatives who work together to ensure that *all* families feel welcome.

Members of a diversity team can read translated written materials to make sure the translation is accurate and appropriate for families in your program. They can help build relationships with families and community members who speak the same home language by planning special events together, or by creating a booklet with information to help everyone understand each other, or by sharing insights about community resources and activities. They might also help to identify culturally and linguistically appropriate books, music, and other learning materials. They may contribute knowledge that builds understanding of languages, cultures, or lifestyles. Most importantly, having an active, engaged diversity team serves as a circle of support for all children, families, and staff.

Members of this group can meet in person or participate in a conference call or other means. They can use skills in their home languages to help spread the word about the way your program welcomes diverse families and volunteers as members of the program community. They can help you and your program find or make culturally and linguistically responsive materials and participate in events and celebrations. A diversity team or committee might provide insights to consider and language to use that inform all staff about welcoming all new families, especially those who speak diverse languages and are from diverse cultures. Interactions with the members of the diversity team encourage ongoing reflection, learning, and change for all staff and members of the school community.

Here are some examples of resources and information community partners on a diversity team might provide:

> The local children's librarian helps you find books and resources that reflect families' languages, cultures, and lifestyles.

> Child care resource and referral agencies share information for families in multiple languages as well as help in obtaining child care funding.

> Cultural organizations, communities of faith, and embassies and consulates offer literature and materials about their countries and cultures.

> Colleges and universities have language and cultural connections, tutors, classroom volunteers, and information.

> United Way, Kiwanis, Rotary, and other service organizations connect you with grants or volunteers.

> Local fairs, festivals, and flea markets sell authentic learning materials that represent the cultures and interests of your community.

> Doctors, dentists, clinics, and social service agencies partner with the program—they need to know about diverse families, and they can offer services to help them thrive.

> An adult education program holds ESL and literacy classes for family members, possibly on site at the program.

In the following example, a diversity team collaborated to meet the needs of bilingual families.

A teacher in a small preschool program in New Jersey noticed a growing population of bilingual families who spoke languages she did not speak. She needed help finding activities, materials, and services for them. The teacher invited families from the school and acquaintances from a local college to get together and brainstorm ideas to expand the program's ability to serve the diverse population of children and families at her school. This small, informal group evolved into an active and effective diversity team. When a new family came to the program, this group stepped in to make them feel welcome right away. They contacted the library and a local church for help in locating books, music, and other items in the family's language. They included these in the program to help the child feel a sense of belonging from the first day.

NAEYC's forthcoming position statement on equity reminds us that our commitment expands beyond a one-time event. It is an ongoing commitment to continuous learning and reflection. The work you do to connect with the community deepens your expertise as an educator and deepens the quality of early childhood education you provide.

Before You Go

Relationships have been and will always be the key component in establishing and maintaining partnerships with families that benefit children. Family engagement efforts are part of the foundation families need to continue to support their children's learning and development. As you continue your journey of building and collaborating with families, consider the reflection questions in each chapter as a guide for your work with families.

Reflection Questions

Now that you have read this chapter, consider the following questions:

1. Which community groups do you have connections with? How do your connections benefit individual families?

2. How do various organizations in your community respond to families' interests, goals, and needs? Which community groups are most helpful; which groups do you and your colleagues want to reach out to?

3. What can you and your colleagues do to help community groups carry out their missions? What are some ways that the program's mission overlaps or complements that of community organizations?

Appendix: Family Engagement Resources

Resources for Educators and Family Support Professionals

The following items are great resources for professionals to use on their own and to share with families. Look for the asterisk (*) for resources that are family-friendly.

Title, Author, Source, & URL	Description	Sample Contents
Abriendo Puertas/Opening Doors: Building a Better Future Through Parent Leadership A Project of the Tides Center Los Angeles, CA www.ap-od.org	This evidence-based comprehensive training program (available in Spanish and English) was developed by and for Latino parents with children ages 0–5. At a three-day institute, facilitators learn to implement the 10 sessions with families.	Best practices are addressed in the following areas: Early childhood development Literacy Numeracy Bilingualism Health Attendance Civic engagement Leadership Goal setting
Building Partnerships: Guide to Developing Relationships with Families National Center on Parent, Family, and Community Engagement https://eclkc.ohs.acf.hhs.gov /sites/default/files/pdf/building -partnerships-developing -relationships-families.pdf (full document)	A professional development guide with learning tools, strategies, and resources for early childhood professionals.	From page 3: The OHS Parent, Family, and Community Engagement Framework is a roadmap for progress. It is a research-based approach to program change designed to help Head Start, Early Head Start, and early childhood programs achieve outcomes that lead to positive and enduring change for children and families.

Title, Author, Source, & URL	Description	Sample Contents
Building Strong Foundations: Advancing Comprehensive Policies for Infants, Toddlers, and Families ZERO TO THREE www.zerotothree.org/resources /series/building-strong-foundations	A collection of resources related to supporting infants, toddlers, and their families.	Some resources in this collection were codeveloped with the Center for Law and Social Policy (CLASP): *From the Ground Up: Establishing Strong Core Policies for Infants, Toddlers, and Families* *Policy Framework for Infants, Toddlers, and Families* *Parent Support Services and Resources: Critical Supports for Infants, Toddlers, and Families*
*Child and Family Blog** Multiple authors University of Cambridge, UK www.childandfamilyblog.com	Developed by The Future of Children at Princeton University and the Applied Developmental Psychology Research Group at the University of Cambridge in 2013 and funded by the Jacobs Foundation in Zurich.	Research-based content includes articles about topics such as: ❯ Flexible work related to fathers' relationships with young children ❯ Grandparents' contributions in families with low incomes ❯ Parent support programs that tackle childhood obesity
Community and Family Toolkit TESOL International Association www.tesol.org/advance-the-field /advocacy-resources/community -and-family-resources-for-elps	This toolkit can be used by English language professionals at all levels to engage families. Each section introduces an effective practice and suggests ways to replicate it. Strategies include a library backpack program, family mentors, family field trips, and information on advocacy efforts.	From "Family Mentors," page 12: Things for You to Consider ❯ Establish how often mentors should check in with mentees. In the beginning, it is advisable that mentors check in once a week. As the year progresses, mentors should check in every other week. ❯ Establish a reporting system of mentor/ mentee meetings and correspondences. ❯ Understand that some mentees may not feel comfortable with additional paperwork. ❯ Consider having mentors write down dates and any issues that need to be resolved. ❯ Consider hosting Family Mentor Program receptions before or after school events to build a community of mentors/mentees.

Title, Author, Source, & URL	Description	Sample Contents
Creating Activities for Strengthening Parent–Child Connections: A Professional's Guide Julia Yeary ZERO TO THREE www.zerotothree.org/resources/25-creating-activities-for-strengthening-parent-child-connections#downloads	Developed as part of *Coming Together Around Military Families*, this guide offers resources and parent–child activities for implementation in a variety of settings.	From activity instructions in the "Story Time" chapter, page 8: Encourage parents to share books with children. Allow children to choose the stories that are shared with them. Volunteers can offer to read a book to the group, if there is an interest. Ideally, however, this would be a chance for parents and children to cuddle and read together.
DEC Recommended Practices Division for Early Childhood of the Council for Exceptional Children Reston, VA 2014 www.dec-sped.org/dec-recommended-practices	This guide informs practitioners and families about the most effective ways to improve the learning outcomes and promote the development of young children, birth through age 5, who have or are at risk for developmental delays or disabilities.	From "Family," page 10: Family practices encompass three themes: 1. **Family-centered practices:** Practices that treat families with dignity and respect; are individualized, flexible, and responsive to each family's unique circumstances; provide family members complete and unbiased information to make informed decisions; and involve family members in acting on choices to strengthen child, parent, and family functioning. 2. **Family capacity-building practices:** Practices that include the participatory opportunities and experiences afforded to families to strengthen existing parenting knowledge and skills and promote the development of new parenting abilities that enhance parenting self-efficacy beliefs and practices. 3. **Family and professional collaboration:** Practices that build relationships between families and professionals who work together to achieve mutually agreed upon outcomes and competencies and support the development of the child.

Title, Author, Source, & URL	Description	Sample Contents
The Early Childhood Family Engagement Framework Toolkit: Maryland's Vision for Engaging Families with Young Children The Maryland Family Engagement Coalition https://c.ymcdn.com/sites /nafsce.site-ym.com/resource /resmgr/Toolkits/Maryland_Early _Childhood_Fam.pdf (full document)	This 98-page comprehensive toolkit outlines Maryland's seven goals for family engagement and approaches to achieving them; addresses special topics such as young dual language learners and cultural proficiency; and shares examples of effective practices, a self-assessment, and resources list.	From Goal 1: Professional Development, page 4: When working with families, relationships should be built on the Three R's: ❯ Receptive—families and staff will listen and be more accepting of what is being said or given to each other. ❯ Responsive—families and staff will react in a positive manner to what is being said or given to each other. Staff and families will be more open to suggestions and sensitive to each other's needs. ❯ Respectful—families and staff will behave in a way that shows regard for each other.
Early Childhood Is Critical to Health Equity Robert Wood Johnson Foundation www.rwjf.org/content/dam/farm /reports/reports/2018/ rwjf445350 (full document)	This 40-page report looks at the health equity of children from birth to age 5. The authors look at conditions that shape lifelong health beginning in the early years and the value of investing in early childhood as a key to health equity.	From page 18: Investments in early childhood must focus not only on providing early care and education services, but also on ensuring that children grow up in health-promoting home, schools, and neighborhoods, which requires addressing poverty and structural racism.
Early Literacy Learning for Immigrant and Refugee Children: Parents' Critical Roles International Literacy Association www.literacyworldwide.org/docs /default-source/where-we-stand /ila-early-literacy-learning -immigrant-refugee-children.pdf (full document)	This Literacy Leadership Brief from the International Literacy Association was created by a panel of more than 20 experts.	Topics include: ❯ Supporting home languages ❯ Cultural models of learning and teaching ❯ How literacy activities and practices differ among families ❯ Code switching ❯ Transferring knowledge across languages
Engaging Families and Creating Trusting Partnerships to Improve Child and Family Outcomes Early Childhood Technical Assistance Center (ECTAC) Frank Porter Graham Child Development Institute University of North Carolina, Chapel Hill March–June 2017 http://ectacenter.org/~calls/2017 /familyengagement.asp	This interactive four-part web broadcast series is a professional development resource for early intervention and early childhood special education specialists. PowerPoint presentation and handouts accompany each segment.	From the handout Principles of Trusting Partnerships, by Rud and Ann Turnbull: Communication involves the verbal, nonverbal, and written messages that partners exchange with each other. ❯ Being friendly ❯ Being clear ❯ Highlighting strengths and good news ❯ Being honest, even with bad news ❯ Responding to feelings ❯ Listening

Title, Author, Source, & URL	Description	Sample Contents
Engaging Families in Early Childhood Education Lily Sanabria-Hernandez RTI (Response to Intervention) Action Network A Program of the National Center for Learning Disabilities www.rtinetwork.org/essential/family/engagingfamilies	This article offers research-based strategies for building reciprocal partnerships with families. While some of the information is targeted to families whose children are at risk for learning disabilities, much of the content is applicable to all families.	In relation to sharing concerns about a child's progress with parents, the author suggests: **Say it again.** For some parents, conversations with school personnel can be stressful, regardless of whether the discussion is about 'good news' or concerns about learning. Try to deliver your message in more than one way, offering examples whenever possible. And ask the listener to confirm what they have heard and what they understand the implications of your message might be. Having parents retell the major points in their own words can be a very helpful strategy to engage parents as partners and to avoid misunderstandings.
Family and Community Engagement US Department of Education www.ed.gov/parent-and-family-engagement	A federal government website offering resources supporting the Department of Education's "framework for building greater support and capacity in schools, homes, and communities, so ALL students have the chance to succeed."	
Family Engagement US Department of Defense's Child Development Virtual Laboratory School (VLS) Developed by The Ohio State University www.virtuallabschool.org/learn (Go to this page and click on the age-specific track you want, and then click on the family engagement course.)	This free online course has five family engagement lessons. Although developed for Department of Defense staff, much of the content applies to any early childhood setting. Content is presented through text and video. Participants read and complete activities in sections, including Know, See, Do, Explore, Apply, and Demonstrate.	To complete Lesson 4, "Working with Families of Children with Special Needs," participants consider their own views: What are some of your own assumptions about families of children with special needs? Download and print the handout Examining Assumptions. Write down some of your reflections. Then you can share your reflections with a trainer, coach, or supervisor.
Family Engagement Toolkit Build Initiative www.buildinitiative.org/Resources/FamilyEngagementToolkit.aspx	A resource collection organized by categories including equity and access, shared decision-making, two-way communication, and sustainability. An overview summarizes the purpose and content of the toolkit. Items are helpful to teachers, families, leaders, and administrators.	

Title, Author, Source, & URL	Description	Sample Contents
Fatherhood Toolkit Multiple authors Parents as Teachers https://parentsasteachers.org/fatherhood-toolkit	According to the mission statement, Parents as Teachers "promotes the optimal early development, learning, and health of children by supporting and engaging their parents and caregivers." The Fatherhood Toolkit offers articles and sample resources related to engaging fathers.	Articles address a variety of topics such as: ❯ The important role fathers play in the lives of young children ❯ Understanding the culture of fathers ❯ Facilitating quality father groups ❯ Great books for dads and kids
Global Family Research Project https://globalfrp.org	This nonprofit organization supports effective family engagement by creating a worldwide exchange of ideas. Articles and other resources are available through the website.	
Head Start Early Childhood Learning and Knowledge Center (ECLKC) Family Engagement https://eclkc.ohs.acf.hhs.gov/family-engagement	This is the landing page for resources and research briefs on the many ways to engage families in their children's early education programming.	From the landing page: Family engagement is a collaborative and strengths-based process through which early childhood professionals, families, and children build positive and goal-oriented relationships. It is a shared responsibility of families and staff at all levels that requires mutual respect for the roles and strengths each has to offer.
Head Start Father Engagement Birth to Five Programming Guide Office of Head Start; the National Center on Parent, Family and Community Engagement; the Early Head Start National Resource Center; and the Head Start Resource Center at Paltech, Inc. June 2013 https://eclkc.ohs.acf.hhs.gov/hslc/tta-system/family/docs/father-engage-programming.pdf (full document)	This 74-page guide covers a range of topics, including leadership, professional development, program environment, partnerships, teaching, and learning. A toolkit offers forms, sample plans, tip sheets, and reflective activities.	From "Program Environment," page 26: Program leadership can work collaboratively with staff—and fathers—to make sure that furniture choice, color schemes, and other aspects of the space are usable and appeal to both women and men. For example, make sure that chairs that fit large frames are available and use inviting colors. Many programs have family rooms where fathers can gather and talk and use computers for job searches. Some offer lending libraries with space for reading to children. Here, young children can engage in positive interactions with men, adding another dimension to a welcoming environment.

Title, Author, Source, & URL	Description	Sample Contents
Head Start Early Childhood Learning and Knowledge Center (ECLKC)* The Importance of Home Language Series https://eclkc.ohs.acf.hhs.gov/culture -language/article/importance-home -language-series	The Importance of Home Language Series focuses on school readiness and school success for children who are dual language learners are tied directly to mastery of their home language. This series of handouts, available in 6 languages, is designed to provide staff and families with basic information on topics related to children learning two or more languages. They emphasize the benefits of being bilingual, the importance of maintaining home language, and the value of becoming fully bilingual. These easy-to-read resources highlight important information that every adult living or working with young dual language learners should know.	From "Language at Home and in the Community, For Families": Here are eight things you can do every day to help your child learn your family's language and become successful in school! 1. Use your language at home: The easiest, most important step is to use your home language every day. Many families worry that using their home language will confuse their children. Actually, children can easily learn several languages at the same time. They have an easier time learning English when they have a strong foundation in their first language.
How to Bring Early Learning and Family Engagement into the Digital Age Lisa Guernsey and Michael H. Levine New America and the Joan Ganz Cooney Center at Sesame Workshop April 2017 www.newamerica.org/education -policy/policy-papers/how-bring -early-learning-and-family -engagement-digital-age	Through infographics and text, this publication describes four actions leaders can take to implement digital learning communities for families. For each step, the authors include examples of communities in action.	Communities-in-action examples include › A project in which Mississippi Public Broadcasting (MPB) collaborated with Dawson Elementary School in Jackson to blend hands-on learning with digital media so families could explore specific topics. › An initiative of the Addison, IL, public library through which both students and parents can get help with online activities.

Title, Author, Source, & URL	Description	Sample Contents
Immigrant Parents and Early Childhood Programs: Addressing Barriers of Literacy, Culture, and Systems Knowledge Maki Park and Margie McHugh Migration Policy Institute June 2014 www.migrationpolicy.org/research/immigrant-parents-early-childhood-programs-barriers	This 62-page report describes the unique needs of parents of young children who are new arrivals to the United States. The content is based on field research in six states, expert interviews, a literature review, and a sociodemographic analysis.	From the Executive Summary: Children of immigrants comprise more than 25 percent of the total US young child population ages 8 and under, requiring an improved understanding of their characteristics and the obstacles they face in achieving educational success. The significant increase in both the share and number of children with at least one foreign-born parent presents a new demographic reality and new challenges for early childhood programs that in many cases are unprepared to meet the needs of these families. Young children of immigrants now make up a significant share of the population across all 50 states in the United States, comprising more than 20 percent of the young child population in 19 states.
The Impact of Family Involvement on the Education of Children Ages 3 to 8: A Focus on Literacy and Math Achievement Outcomes and Social-Emotional Skills Francis L. Van Voorhis, Michelle F. Maier, Joyce L. Epstein, and Chrishana M. Lloyd MDRC October 2013 www.mdrc.org/sites/default/files/The_Impact_of_Family_Involvement_FR.pdf (full document)	This 229-page report "summarizes research conducted primarily over the past 10 years on how families' involvement in children's learning and development through activities at home and at school affects the literacy, mathematics, and social-emotional skills of children ages 3 to 8."	From Key Findings: ❯ Family involvement is important for young children's literacy and math skills. ❯ Parents from diverse backgrounds, when given direction, can become more engaged with their children. And when parents are more engaged, children tend to do better.

Title, Author, Source, & URL	Description	Sample Contents
Learning with PBS KIDS: A Study of Family Engagement and Early Mathematics Achievement Betsy McCarthy, Linlin Li, Michelle Tiu, Sara Atienza, and Ursula Sexton WestEd November 2015 www.wested.org/wp-content /uploads/2016/11/1446854213 resourcelearningwithpbskids-3.pdf (full document)	A 62-page report on a study of family engagement and early mathematics learning as part of the Ready To Learn (RTL) Initiative with the Corporation for Public Broadcasting (CPB) and the Public Broadcasting Service (PBS). The study was designed to test the effectiveness of a school-based family engagement model in increasing preschoolers' knowledge and skills in mathematics, and in increasing parents' awareness of and ability to support their children's mathematics learning in the home environment.	From "Themes from Qualitative Data Analysis," page 35, parent comments included: Now it's more in my head for how to [help] her to learn. Like, we'd be around the house, "Do you know what shape this is?" and she'll say, "Square!" And now I'm trying to figure out a way for her to get to 3-D from the flat. So I tell her, "It looks like a square at the bottom and on the top and the side, but you can put something inside. It's not flat." I say, "It looks like a square, but can you put something inside?" She'll say, "Yes," so I'm like, "Well, what shape is it then?" She says, "A cube."
Mindset Shifts and Parent Teacher Home Visits Katherine McKnight, Nitya Venkateswaran, Jennifer Laird, Jessica Robles, and Talia Shalev RTI International October 2017 www.pthvp.org/wp-content /uploads/2018/12/171030-Mindset ShiftsandPTHVReportFINAL.pdf	This 64-page report summarizes findings from a study of whether the Parent Teacher Home Visit model helps to interrupt biases held by educators and families. Researchers considered mindsets related to race, class, and culture.	Regarding holding parent teacher meetings in a neutral location, on page 27, researchers learned: ❯ Meeting outside the school, in a place that is comfortable for families, allowed school staff to see things they hadn't seen before in on-campus interactions. ❯ Meeting outside the school shifts the traditional power dynamic between schools and families to more equal footing.
The National Association for Family, School and Community Engagement (NAFSCE) https://nafsce.site-ym.com	The mission of this membership organization is: "To advance high-impact policies and practices for family, school, and community engagement to promote child development and improve student achievement." A searchable resource library offers some materials for all users and some for members only. Sign up to receive a twice-monthly newsletter.	From an interview with Harvard faculty member and NAFSCE Board Member Karen Mapp, conducted by Neal Morton: **Q:** For families who feel they aren't welcome or respected at schools, what are some of the more effective ways educators can reengage with them? **A:** First of all, there are very few families who I would say are completely lost and we're not able to reach. But it takes persistence. And it takes patience. What parents want to see is that you love their children.

Title, Author, Source, & URL	Description	Sample Contents
National Center on Parent, Family, and Community Engagement (NCPFCE) Professional Development Guide Boston Children's Hospital Brazleton Touchpoints Center, in collaboration with Child Care Aware of America, the Center for the Study of Social Policy, and Child Trends The Office of Head Start and the Office of Child Care https://eclkc.ohs.acf.hhs.gov/pdguide	A comprehensive digital guide for Head Start, Early Head Start, and early child care programs that provides professional development resources organized by content areas. Users can learn about an overall approach, relationships, family engagement and school readiness, and leadership and program practices.	From the Understanding Family Engagement Outcomes: Research to Practice Series, "Family Engagement in Transitions: Transition to Kindergarten": Programs can help families of dual language learners learn about their rights. Programs can also provide relevant information in the preferred languages of families, as well as English. All families need to feel empowered to exercise these rights and to seek out the community resources they need to do so. . . . Knowing these rights and successfully advocating for them in a new school can be difficult. Strong staff–family partnerships can help.
*National Fatherhood Initiative** Germantown, MD www.fatherhood.org	Find digital apps and other resources supporting father engagement. A Father-Friendly Check-Up Tool lets schools and programs assess their support for equitable participation of fathers.	
National Standards for Family–School Partnerships: Implementation Guide National PTA 2009 www.pta.org/home/run-your-pta/National-Standards-for-Family-School-Partnerships	Three steps: ❯ Raising awareness about the power of family and community involvement. ❯ Taking action to cultivate involvement through specific programs and practices. ❯ Celebrating success as your school sees increased involvement and its impact. Assessment tool for each step and implementation guide.	From page 33: For the standard of collaborating with community, there is one overriding goal: connecting the school with community resources. Parent and school leaders should work closely with neighborhood associations, government agencies, businesses, and institutions of higher education to strengthen the school. These collaborations should make resources available to students, school staff, and families and build a family-friendly community.
Opening Doors for Young Parents, KIDS COUNT Policy Report Anny E. Casey Foundation Baltimore, MD 2018 www.aecf.org/m/resourcedoc/aecf-openingdoorsforyoungparents-2018.pdf (full document)	Shares current data and analyses of the barriers young families face, using national- and state-level trends. Authors highlight areas of opportunity and concern, along with potential solutions.	From the Introduction, page 2: Young people are the workers of today and tomorrow. But those who become parents in their teenage years and early 20s, just as they are getting started in the world of work, are often confronted with a harsh reality: odds stacked against their ability to earn, learn, and raise a family, which can threaten their children's future as well as the strength of our communities.

Title, Author, Source, & URL	Description	Sample Contents
Parent Engagement Practices Improve Outcomes for Preschool Children Karen Bierman, Pamela Morris, and Rachel Abenavoli Robert Wood Johnson Foundation and Pennsylvania State University January 2017 www.rwjf.org/content/dam/farm /reports/issue_briefs/2017 /rwjf432769 (full document)	This 10-page issue brief documents the "promise and challenge" of engaging families in which young children are at risk for not being ready for school. Several effective family engagement models are highlighted.	From "Key Findings," page 5: If preschool-based efforts do not attract disadvantaged families and if they do not successfully increase the parent attitudes and behaviors that directly affect child development, they will not improve child school readiness or reduce socioeconomic disparities in school readiness and success.
Partners in Education: A Dual Capacity-Building Framework for Family–School Partnerships Karen L. Mapp and Paul J. Kuttner SEDL for the US Department of Education 2013 www2.ed.gov/documents/family -community/partners-education. pdf (full document)	This 28-page paper presents a research-based framework for designing family engagement initiatives. Three case studies demonstrate how educational systems have implemented the framework at a school, district, and county levels.	From Case 3, First 5 Santa Clara County, page 22, teacher Jan White comments: I have gained an amazing amount of respect for what our parents go through, and I have to say I'm not sure I could overcome many of the obstacles that they overcame. I highly respect what they do, and even though it may not always be the way I do it, or the way I would do it, or how I think they should do it, I don't think I've met a parent yet who wouldn't do whatever they could to help their child do better in school. They just don't always know how. I have grown to love and respect these parents very much. That's why I don't leave.
PBS Parents* www.pbs.org/parents	This site, available in English and Spanish, provides a diverse array of information on child development and early learning and access to games, activities, and other materials that build on the learning experiences embedded in PBS KIDS programs. Items are categorized by age, making it accessible.	From "Stay on Track with Healthy Snacks": Choosing and Buying Snacks › Buy only healthy snacks, such as fruits and vegetables. › Before you go shopping, tell your children what behavior you expect and what, if any, snack they can expect. › Take snacks with you when you go to appointments or run errands. › Provide snacks that are easy to eat. › Use snacks to provide the food groups your children are missing during meals. › Make snacks small, then give seconds if the child asks for more. › Decide what snacks you will allow, and when. Explain the rules to your child and stick to them.

Title, Author, Source, & URL	Description	Sample Contents
Principles of Effective Family Engagement NAEYC's Engaging Diverse Families Project NAEYC.org/resources/topics/family -engagement/principles	Developed as part of a study that defined successful family engagement, identified exemplary family engagement practices in early childhood programs, and shared what was learned by assembling a toolkit of materials to help programs more effectively engage families in children's early learning.	
Raising Young Children in a New Country: Supporting Early Learning and Healthy Development* The Office of Head Start and the Office of Refugee Resettlement Retrieved February 2019 https://eclkc.ohs.acf.hhs.gov /sites/default/files/pdf/raising -young-children-new-country.pdf	This handbook (available in four languages) provides prenatal and early childhood information for refugee families. Through diverse illustrations and brief, but important, content, refugee families learn about health, safety, routines, guidance, brain development, and early learning, and family engagement in early childhood programs and schools.	In the section on early learning and school readiness, families learn that 3- to 5-year-old children progress when they: Use home language at home. Use home language and English at school. Use a variety of words in both languages. Sing songs, learn rhymes, and tell stories in both languages. Ask children to tell you stories in both languages. Provide books with pictures, short stories, rhymes, poems, and alphabet books in both languages. Offer markers, crayons, pencils, and paper to encourage drawing and to imitate writing.

Title, Author, Source, & URL	Description	Sample Contents
Ripples of Transformation: Families Leading Change in Early Childhood Systems *A Family Engagement Toolkit for Providers and Program Leaders* Melia Franklin First 5 Alameda County, CA www.cssp.org/wp-content /uploads/2018/08/FirstFive -EngagementToolkit-5.pdf (full document)	Three sections in this guide cover: 1. **Engaging with their children:** Families enhance their role as the child's "first teacher" through learning about their child's development, building a network, and getting support for basic needs and parenting challenges. 2. **Shaping programs and services:** Families partner with organizations to inform decisions, participate in planning and delivery of services, and become leaders. 3. **Influencing policies and systems:** Families use their voices and experiences to advocate for improved, family-centered, equity-driven systems, programs and services.	From "Families Influencing Policies and Systems," page 15: One parent relates: "I am representing others by telling my story on committees." Another parent points out that to be an advocate is to move from a focus on "my child" to "my community": "I raise my voice as a parent leader . . . not only for my daughter, it is for the other students, the other children, and even for the teachers and staff themselves."
Services for Families of Infants and Toddlers Experiencing Trauma Brenda Jones Harden US Department of Health and Human Services, Office of Planning, Research, and Evaluation www.acf.hhs.gov/opre/resource /impact-of-trauma-families -of-infants-and-toddlers	This 16-page research brief reviews what is known about the impact of trauma on infants and toddlers. The author describes intervention strategies that could be helpful, with a focus on interventions that support parents in providing stable and nurturing caregiving. In addition, there is a discussion of the role of delivery systems such as Early Head Start, home visiting, and child welfare programs.	From "Promising Interventions for Infants and Toddlers," page 8: Trauma-Adapted Family Connections (TAFC) . . . is delivered in the home, usually via one session per week for six months. The intervention uses family therapy, cognitive-behavioral strategies, and case management to address trauma, family stressors and crises, and environmental risk factors. Given that TAFC includes children of all ages in the family who experience trauma, it would be important to ensure that practitioners using this model serve infants and toddlers using developmentally appropriate strategies.

Title, Author, Source, & URL	Description	Sample Contents
State Approaches to Family Engagement in Pre-K Programs Melissa Dahlin, MA Center on Enhancing Early Learning Outcomes (CEELO) March 2016 http://ceelo.org/wp-content /uploads/2016/03/ceelo_policy _brief_family_engagement _2016_03_final_web_updated _2016_11.pdf (full document)	This 31-page policy brief draws on work CEELO completed while working with two states to develop guidance on family engagement. The brief discusses why family engagement is important, approaches to developing guidance for programs, and strategies for effective implementation.	In "Program Standards," page 9: Successful strategies are attuned to and responsive to the culture and desires of the families and the context and values of the community where the program lives. Therefore, it is critical to design standards in a way that programs or schools can adhere to them while also having the flexibility to tailor their approach to meet the goals of the families in their community.
Understanding Family Engagement Outcomes: Research to Practice Series Office of Head Start National Center on Parent, Family, and Community Engagement (NCPFCE) https://eclkc.ohs.acf.hhs.gov /family-engagement/article /understanding-family-engagement -outcomes-research-practice-series	The Research to Practice Series presents a summary of selected research, proven interventions and promising practices, and program strategies. Topics addressed include family well-being, parental depression, families as learners, school readiness, parent–child relationships, lifelong learning, transition to kindergarten, peer and community support systems, and advocacy and leadership.	From *Family Well-Being*, page 4: Challenges to family well-being can be especially difficult when they occur together and build up over time. When parents are overwhelmed, their hope and motivation may waver. Programs can use their unique, two-generational model to reenergize families through their passion for their children. Programs can then help families develop strategies to protect or restore family well-being. Programs can also combine respectful, goal-oriented family partnerships with strong connections to community resource providers to support overall family well-being.

Resources for Families

The following resources are designed and written with families in mind as the target audience.

Title, Author, Source, & URL	Description	Sample Contents
Child and Family WebGuide WebGuide managers: W. George Scarlett, John Hornstein, Kathryn Dietz, Dianne Brown, and William Hilley School of Arts and Sciences Tufts University www.ase.tufts.edu/cfw	To counteract the preponderance of erroneous information on the Internet, this offers parents and families a collection of websites that have been carefully reviewed and deemed to be trustworthy. A variety of topics are addressed related to development, education and schooling, physical and mental health, and parents and families.	Topics addressed under development include brain development, stuttering, gender identity development, motor skills, and self-esteem. Topics addressed under education and schooling include early intervention, multicultural literature, nature, bullying, and bilingual education.
Family Engagement Toolkit BUILD Initiative www.buildinitiative.org/Resources/FamilyEngagementToolkit.aspx	This toolkit offers resources for families, teachers, principals, and district leaders. Content covers topics such as shared decision-making, building partnerships, sharing data with families, and child portfolios.	From *Your Family Has a Voice*: As a member of the school community, you have an important role in your child's learning. Keep in mind that you have the right to: ❯ Ask questions about your child's learning ❯ Participate in classroom activities and events ❯ Share any concerns you have about your child's growth or learning ❯ Share information about any changes you've noticed in your child's development ❯ Share any information that you think would help the teacher work better with your child ❯ Ask for privacy; sensitive or confidential information about your family should not be shared with the larger school community ❯ Ask that the school provide you with information that is clear and easy to understand ❯ Ask that information be made available to you in your home language ❯ Ask that your child be assessed/screened if you are concerned about your child's growth and development ❯ Ask for a conference or meeting with your child's teacher to discuss any concerns

Title, Author, Source, & URL	Description	Sample Contents
For Families National Association for the Education of Young Children (NAEYC) NAEYC.org/our-work/for-families	This area of the NAEYC website includes research-based resources, tips, and ideas for families. Topics include young children's development in all domains and sections focused on literacy, math, music, and more.	From "10 Ways Babies Learn When We Sing to Them," by Cathy Fink and Marcy Marxer: 1. **Bonding** – When you sing to your baby, they bond with you and your voice. Singing makes yours the first and most important voice in her life. Your baby learns that you LOVE him! 2. **Transitions** – Babies feel safe when life is predictable. A song for waking up, sleeping, and other routine transitions and activities helps them know what comes next. 3. **Language** – Language is in itself musical, and when you sing and speak, your baby learns about words, language, and communication. Through your singing, baby's language comprehension begins.
Reading Rockets www.readingrockets.org	Families can subscribe to Growing Readers, a free monthly newsletter offering tips for parents. In addition, the web page features resources on early literacy, books, partnering with schools, family literacy activities, supporting children with learning disabilities, and more.	From "How to Read an E-Book with Your Child" Electronic books are becoming more and more commonplace. Here you'll discover practical tips for sharing e-books with your child, and how to keep the focus on reading and the story. Electronic books, called e-books, are becoming more and more commonplace these days. Some readers, like the first generation Kindle and Nook devices, offer a basic digital version of a print book. Children scroll through the pages to read, and the experience is somewhat similar to reading a traditional book.
Ready Rosie Denton, TX www.readyrosie.com	Available by organizational subscription, this tool helps families, schools, and communities implement family engagement strategies. In Spanish and English versions, articles, short videos, and modeling encourage developmentally appropriate practice.	

Title, Author, Source, & URL	Description	Sample Contents
Ready4Routines: Building the Skills for Mindful Parenting Center for the Developing Child, Harvard University https://developingchild.harvard.edu/resources/ready4routines-building-the-skills-for-mindful-parenting/	The video on this webpage is part of a larger project that helps families build regular routines. Using real-life daily events such as bedtime and mealtime, the focus is on increasing predictability for young children and strengthening executive function skills in adults and children.	
Sesame Street in Communities Sesame Street www.sesamestreetincommunities.org	This site offers multimedia resources in English and Spanish for families and caregivers of children from birth to age 6. There are printable handouts for adults to use with children. Topics include school readiness, health, and tender topics such as divorce and trauma. A section for educators includes professional development resources.	From "Breathe, Balance, and Bend: The 3 B's of Calm Bodies": Breathing deeply and slowly is a calming strategy for anytime, anywhere. ❯ Ask children to place their hands over their mouths and feel their breath. Together, breathe quickly, then slowly, and ask children to compare how each breath feels in their hands. ❯ Then ask children to pretend their bellies are balloons. Encourage them to take long and deep breaths to fill the balloons with air, then breathe out through their mouths to let the air out.
Too Small to Fail Joint initiative of the Clinton Foundation and The Opportunity Institute www.toosmall.org	This public awareness and action campaign promotes early brain and language development and empowers parents with tools to talk, read, and sing with their young children from birth. Parents can sign up to receive resources via email.	From "Talking Is Teaching: READ": ❯ Read a book or tell a story to your baby every day—in whatever language you feel most comfortable—beginning at birth. ❯ Cuddle with your baby as you share a book. It doesn't matter how young your child is; even newborn babies are learning when their parents read with them. ❯ Point to the book's pictures: "Look, the train goes choo-choo!" Using words to describe what you see builds language.

Title, Author, Source, & URL	Description	Sample Contents
ZERO TO THREE Washington, DC www.zerotothree.org	This nonprofit organization has a rich array of videos and written resources about the development and care of infants and toddlers. Parents can sign up for an age-based newsletter. Topics include early development and well-being, early learning, parenting, and policy and advocacy. The website's Parenting area is "designed to support parents in developing their own ways to promote their children's growth and development."	From the landing page of Parent Favorites, a collection of 11 most popular resources: There is no such thing as a perfect parent. Parenting is an ongoing process of learning who your individual child is and what he needs to thrive

Digital Resources for Families

Let's Play!

ZERO TO THREE

A free parenting app, available on the iTunes store, with early learning activities, organized by age and routine, for parents and young children to use together.

Ready4K

Parent-Powered Technologies

https://ready4k.parentpowered.com

Developed by Stanford-trained educational researchers, this free app is for parents of children from birth to third grade. Activities build on typical home routines.

Text4Baby

Wellpass

https://partners.text4baby.org/index.php

This app focuses on the prenatal period and the baby's first year of life. Through a partnership with Sesame Street and Too Small to Fail, they offer child development tips and videos.

Model Family Engagement Approaches

Avance: Parent-Child Education Program

San Antonio, TX

www.avance.org/programs

With sites located in Texas and California, Avance focuses on its mission of "unlocking America's potential by strengthening families in at-risk communities through effective parent education and support programs." They focus on families and children from birth to age 3. "The key to healthy early childhood development begins with capitalizing on parents' inner strength and innate love for their children to help them become the best teachers and stewards of their children's growth and success. Parental education alone is not enough; an effective intervention must build parents' resilience, interpersonal connections, networks, and access to education, jobs, and other opportunities. True parental engagement empowers parents to become advocates for their children and families."

Family Place Libraries

www.familyplacelibraries.org

This national network includes children's librarians in 29 US states. Through its 450 sites, the program acknowledges that literacy learning begins in infancy. Public libraries become community centers for early literacy and learning, family education and engagement, family support, and community connections. Administrators and staff take part in an institute and online training on providing program services where they learn about child development, family support, parent education, and best practices.

Family Place libraries offer a five-week series of parent–child workshops, provides special collections and spaces that support early literacy explorations for children from birth through age 5, collaborates with other agencies, and identifies and reaches out to new and underserved families. A list of family place sites appears on the website.

Harlem Children's Zone

https://hcz.org

Harlem Children's Zone is an educational and community services program in Harlem, NY. Its comprehensive approach supports children from birth through college and their families.

Support for Families of Children with Disabilities

www.supportforfamilies.org

This is a parent-run organization that offers free information, education, and parent-to-parent support for "families of children with any kind of disability or special health care need." They serve families and early educators in San Francisco.

State Approaches to Family Engagement

Alabama. The state's early childhood initiative, Strong Start, Strong Finish, includes Strong Families = A Strong Start to encourage family engagement. This initiative addresses the school readiness gap by promoting home visiting programs that have helped parents become effective "first teachers" for their children. http://children.alabama.gov

Arizona. The Arizona Department of Education Family Engagement Initiative is a cross-division effort to build and strengthen partnerships between families and schools to enhance student achievement. www.azed.gov/21stcclc /family-engagement

California. The California Department of Education provides a list of links to its state Family Engagement Framework and other tools for schools and districts, including a guide to Title I School–Parent Compacts and *The Family Engagement Framework: A Tool for California School Districts*. www.cde.ca.gov/ls/pf/pf

Colorado. In 2009, Colorado passed legislation adopting the PTA National Standards as the framework schools should use for family engagement: www.pta.org/home/run-your-pta /National-Standards-for-Family-School-Partnerships. Colorado offers an extensive list of training and information materials on promising practices in family engagement (www.cde.state.co.us/uip/trainingmaterials) and a brochure developed by the Colorado Department of Education and the State Advisory Council on Parent Involvement in Education to raise awareness about family–school partnerships. www.cde.state.co.us/sacpie/sacpiebrochure91014

Connecticut. The Connecticut State Department of Education has pioneered a new approach to creating Title I School–Parent Compacts that is being adopted by other states such as California and Georgia. Learn about their 10-step approach, with video information and tools for each step on a special website. http://ctschoolparentcompact.org

Illinois. The Illinois Board of Education has developed a comprehensive framework for family engagement, described in a Family Engagement Guide. The guide combines research and best practices with legislative requirements, and it provides resources that integrate family engagement into the school improvement process. It can be used to develop and expand school-family partnerships to support student learning and healthy development. www.isbe.net/Pages/Family-Engagement -Framework-Guide.aspx

Maryland. The Maryland Family Engagement Coalition and the Maryland State Department of Education, Division of Early Childhood Development, created *The Early Childhood Family Engagement Framework Toolkit: Maryland's Vision for Engaging Families with Young Children* as part of the Family Engagement Initiative, funded by the W.K. Kellogg Foundation. This toolkit is geared for Maryland's early childhood community as they implement strategies to promote family engagement and to improve families and children's outcomes by promoting a two-generational approach. https://earlychildhood. marylandpublicschools.org/system/files/filedepot/4 /md_fam_engage.pdf

Blogs and Short Articles

Analysis: 4 Steps Schools Can Take to Boost Family Engagement and Make Parents Partners in Their Kids' Success
Jessica Lander
The 74
November 2017
www.the74million.org/article/analysis-4-steps-schools-can-take-to-boost-family-engagement-and-make-parents-partners-in-their-kids-success

Count on Families! Engaging Families in Math
Margaret Caspe
Global Family Research Project
August 2017
https://globalfrp.org/Articles/Count-on-Families!-Engaging-Families-in-Math

How Can Schools Tap into Parent Power for the Good of Students?
Zaidee Stavely
KQED News
MindShift
January 25, 2016
ww2.kqed.org/mindshift/2016/01/25/how-can-schools-tap-into-parent-power-for-the-good-of-students

How to Communicate with Parents
ZERO TO THREE
February 2010
www.zerotothree.org/resources/92-how-to-communicate-with-parents

Lessons Learned from Our Collaborations with Families
Aaron Miller
NAEYC
April 10, 2017
NAEYC.org/resources/blog/lessons-learned-our-collaborations-families

Message in a Backpack
Teaching Young Children
NAEYC
NAEYC.org/search/Message%20in%20a%20Backpack?f%5B0%5D=field_topics%3A174

Modern Families: What Educators Need to Know
Brenda Álvarez
December 19, 2013
National Education Association
http://neatoday.org/2013/12/19/modern-families-what-educators-need-to-know-2

News: Educare Schools Build Strong Relationships with Parents
Educare Learning Network
October 12, 2015
www.educareschools.org/educare-schools-build-strong-relationships-with-parents

Partnering with Newcomer Families: Strategies for Working Across Language and Cultural Differences to Make Families Feel at Home in New Schools
Leah Shafer
Harvard Graduate School of Education
April 26, 2018
www.gse.harvard.edu/news/uk/18/04/partnering-newcomer-families

Six Shifts for Better Family Engagement
Search Institute
June 15, 2017
www.search-institute.org/blog/6-shifts-for-better-family-engagement

Stages of Immigrant Parent Involvement— Survivors to Leaders
Phi Beta Kappan
Young-chan Han and Jennifer Love
August 15, 2016
www.kappanonline.org/stages-of-immigrant-parent-involvement-survivors-to-leaders

Supporting Children in Immigrant Families: A Back-to-School Checklist for Educators
CLASP
Rebecca Ullrich
September 8, 2017
www.clasp.org/blog/supporting-children-immigrant-families-back-school-checklist-educators

Books, Booklets, and Brochures

Adair, J., & J. Tobin. 2008. "Listening to the Voices of Immigrant Parents." *In Diversities in Early Childhood Education: Rethinking and Doing,* eds. C. Genishi & A.L. Goodwin, 137–50. New York: Routledge.

Byington, T. 2018. *Raising a Reader, Raising a Writer: Tips for Families*. Rev. ed. Brochure. Washington, DC: NAEYC.

California Department of Education (CDE) & WestEd. 2010. *A Guide to Creating Partnerships with Families*. 2nd ed. Sacramento: CDE.

Dotsch, J. 2013. *Supporting the Settlement of Young Immigrant Children and Their Families: A Guide for Early Childhood Educators*. Ontario, Canada: GCS, Inc.

Galinsky, E. 1987. *The Six Stages of Parenthood*. New York: Perseus Books.

Genishi, C., & A.L. Goodwin, eds. 2008. *Diversities in Early Childhood Education: Rethinking and Doing*. New York: Routledge.

Gillanders, C., I. Iruka, C. Bagwell, J. Morgan, & S.C. García. 2014. "Home and School Partnerships: Raising Children Together." Chap. 6 in *First School: Transforming PreK–3rd Grade for African American, Latino, and Low-Income Children,* eds. S. Ritchie & L. Gutmann, 125–48. New York: Teachers College Press

Gonzalez-Mena, J. 2013. *50 Strategies for Communicating and Working with Diverse Families*. 3rd ed. Boston: Pearson.

Hanson, M.J., & E.W. Lynch. 2013. *Understanding Families: Supportive Approaches to Diversity, Disability, and Risk*. 2nd ed. Baltimore: Brookes.

Henderson, A.T., K.L. Mapp, V.R. Johnson, & D. Davies. 2007. *Beyond the Bake Sale: The Essential Guide to Family–School Partnerships*. New York: The New Press.

Lally, J.R., P.L. Mangione, & D. Greenwald, eds. 2006. *Concepts for Care: 20 Essays on Infant/Toddler Development and Learning*. San Francisco: WestEd.

LeeKeenan, D., & I.C. Ponte. 2018. *From Survive to Thrive: A Director's Guide for Leading an Early Childhood Program*. Washington, DC: NAEYC.

Mapp, K.L., I. Carver, & J. Lander. 2017. *Powerful Partnerships: A Teacher's Guide to Engaging Families for Student Success*. New York: Scholastic.

NAEYC. 2017. *A High Quality Program for Your Infant*. Brochure. Washington, DC: NAEYC.

NAEYC. 2017. *A High Quality Program for Your Preschooler*. Brochure. Washington, DC: NAEYC.

NAEYC. 2017. *A High Quality Program for Your Toddler*. Brochure. Washington, DC: NAEYC.

NAEYC. 2017. *A High Quality School for Your Kindergartner*. Brochure. Washington, DC: NAEYC.

NAEYC. 2017. *A High Quality School for Your Child in First, Second, or Third Grade*. Brochure. Washington, DC: NAEYC.

NAEYC. 2016. *The What, Why, and How of High-Quality Programs for Infants*. Booklet. Washington, DC: NAEYC.

NAEYC. 2016. *The What, Why, and How of High-Quality Programs for Preschoolers*. Booklet. Washington, DC: NAEYC.

NAEYC. 2016. *The What, Why, and How of High-Quality Programs for Toddlers*. Booklet. Washington, DC: NAEYC.

NAEYC. 2016. *The What, Why, and How of High-Quality School for Kindergartners*. Booklet. Washington, DC: NAEYC.

NAEYC. 2016. *The What, Why, and How of High-Quality School for Children in First, Second, and Third Grades*. Booklet. Washington, DC: NAEYC.

National Academies of Sciences, Engineering, and Medicine. 2016. *Parenting Matters: Supporting Parents of Children Ages 0–8*. Washington DC: The National Academies Press. doi:10.17226/21868.

Nixon, A.S., & K.D. Gutierrez. 2008. "Digital Literacies for Young English Learners: Productive Pathways Toward Equity and Robust Learning." In *Diversities in Early Childhood Education: Rethinking and Doing,* eds. C. Genishi & A.L. Goodwin, 121–36. New York: Routledge.

Owen, S., & S. Owen, eds. 2005. *Authentic Relationships in Group Care for Infants and Toddlers—Resources for Infant Educarers (RIE): Principles into Practice*. Philadelphia: Jessica Kingsley Publishers.

Pepper, A. 2017. *Kick-Start Kindergarten Readiness*. Lewiston, NC: Gryphon House.

Tobin, J., A.E. Arzubiaga, & J.K. Adair. 2013. *Children Crossing Borders: Immigrant Parent and Teacher Perspectives on Preschool*. New York: Russell Sage Foundation.

Ward, U. 2013. *Working with Parents in the Early Years*. 2nd ed. Thousand Oaks, CA: Sage.

Journal articles

Belz, P. 2017. "Following Parents and Children into the Forest: A Visit to the Berkeley Forest School." *Exchange* 39 (5): 60–63.

Breiseth, L. 2016. "Getting to Know ELLs' Families." *Educational Leadership* 73 (5): 46–50.

Doucette, A. 2015."The Building Blocks of Family Engagement." *Teaching Young Children* 9 (2): 26–28.

Hilado, A.V., L. Kallemeyn, & L. Phillips. 2013. "Examining Understandings of Parent Involvement in Early Childhood Programs." *Early Childhood Research and Practice* 15 (2). www.ecrp.uiuc.edu/v15n2/hilado.html.

Julius, G.D. 2017. "The Importance of Parent-Provider Relationships in Early Education." *Exchange* 39 (5): 48–50.

Morland, L., & T. Levine. 2016. "Collaborating with Refugee Resettlement Organizations: Providing a Head Start to Young Refugees." *Young Children* 71 (4): 69–75.

Muccio, L.S., R. Kuwahara-Fujita, & J.J.Y. Otsuji. 2015."Ohana Math: Family Engagement to Encourage Math Learning at Home." *Teaching Young Children* 9 (2): 10–13.

Mwenelupembe, A. 2017. "Filling in the Gaps: Empowering Parents' Understanding of Play to Support School Readiness." *Exchange* 39 (5): 54–56.

Pack, J. 2015. "Learning Stories." *Teaching Young Children* 9 (2): 18–21.

Parnell, W., E. Justice, & L. P. Patrick. 2018. "Engaging Extended Family and Friends in Young Children's Education." *Young Children* 73 (4): 20–27.

Peterson, A.A., L.J. Dooley, & L. Fan. 2018. "Home Visiting Programs: Supporting Relationships and Healthy Development." *Young Children* 73 (4): 36–41.

Stewart-Henry, K., & A. Friesen. 2018."Promoting Powerful Interactions Between Parents and Children." *Teaching Young Children* 11 (5): 24–27.

Swartz, R.A. 2017. "Welcoming Families Receiving Early Intervention Services into Your Early Childhood Program." *Exchange* 39 (5): 51–53.

Thompson, H. 2015. "Explaining Developmentally Appropriate Practice to Families." *Teaching Young Children* 9 (2): 16–17.

Vesely, C.K., & M.R. Ginsberg. 2011. "Strategies and Practices for Working with Immigrant Families in Early Education Programs." *Young Children* 66 (1): 84–89.

Vesely, C.K., E.L. Brown, & S. Mehta. 2017. "Developing Cultural Humility Through Experiential Learning: How Home Visits Transform Early Childhood Preservice Educators' Attitudes for Engaging Families." *Journal of Early Childhood Teacher Education* 38 (3): 242–58.

Woodman, T. 2017. "A Community of Eaters: Bringing Families Together Through a Classroom Food Blog." *Exchange* 39 (5): 57–59.

References

Annie E. Casey Foundation. 2018. *Opening Doors for Young Parents*. KIDS COUNT policy report. Baltimore: Annie E. Casey Foundation. www.aecf.org /resources/opening-doors-for-young-parents.

Barrueco, S., S. Smith, & S.A. Stephens. 2016. "Supporting Parent Engagement in Linguistically Diverse Families to Promote Young Children's Life Success." *Journal of Applied Research on Children: Informing Policy for Children at Risk* 7 (1): Article 13. https://digitalcommons.library.tmc.edu /childrenatrisk/vol7/iss1/13.

Bierman, K.L., P.A. Morris, & R.M. Abenavoli. 2017. "Parent Engagement Practices Improve Outcomes for Preschool Children." Issue brief. University Park, PA: Edna Bennett Pierce Prevention Research Center, Pennsylvania State University. www.rwjf.org /en/library/research/2017/02/parent-engagement -practices-improve-outcomes-for-preschool-child.html.

Bulotsky-Shearer, R.J., X. Wen, A.M. Faria, D.L. Hahs-Vaughn, & J. Korfmacher. 2012. "National Profiles of Classroom Quality and Family Involvement: A Multilevel Examination of Proximal Influences on Head Start Children's School Readiness." *Early Childhood Research Quarterly* 27 (1): 627–639.

Celano, D.C., & S.B. Neuman. 2015. "Libraries Emerging as Leaders in Parent Engagement." *Phi Delta Kappan* 96 (7): 30–35.

Center for Plain Language. n.d. Richmond, VA: Center for Plain Language. www.centerforplainlanguage.org.

Child Care Aware of America. n.d. "The State of Family Engagement in Quality Rating and Improvement System Efforts." Brief. Arlington: VA. Child Care Aware of America. http://usa.childcareaware.org/wp -content/uploads/2016/05/FamilyEngagementBrief _final.pdf.

Christakis, E. 2018. "The Dangers of Distracted Parenting." *The Atlantic*, July/August. www .theatlantic.com/magazine/archive/2018/07/the -dangers-of-distracted-parenting/561752.

Children's Bureau. n.d. "Benefits of Community Involvement in Early Childhood." www.all4kids.org /2018/03/02/benefits-of-community-involvement -in-early-childhood.

Copple, C., & S. Bredekamp, eds. 2009. *Developmentally Appropriate Practice in Early Childhood Programs Serving Children from Birth through Age 8*. 3rd ed. Washington, DC: NAEYC.

Derman-Sparks, L., D. LeeKeenan, & J. Nimmo. 2015. *Leading Anti-Bias Early Childhood Programs: A Guide for Change*. New York: Teachers College Press.

Donohue, C., ed. 2016. *Family Engagement in the Digital Age: Early Childhood Educators as Media Mentors*. New York: Routledge.

Educare Learning Network. 2015. "Educare Schools Build Strong Relationships with Parents." www .educareschools.org/educare-schools-build-strong -relationships-with-parents.

Edwards, N.M. 2018. "Family Feedback and Programmatic Decision-Making: Responsiveness of Early Childhood Administrators." *Early Childhood Education Journal* 46 (4): 397–407.

Edwards, P.A. 2016. *New Ways to Engage Parents: Strategies and Tools for Teachers and Leaders, K–12*. New York: Teachers College Press.

Feeney, S., & N.K. Freeman. 2018. *Ethics and the Early Childhood Educator: Using the NAEYC Code*. 3rd ed. Washington, DC: NAEYC.

Gonzalez-Mena, J. 2013. *Child, Family, and Community: Family-Centered Early Care and Education*. 6th ed. Upper Saddle River, NJ: Pearson.

Gross, N., & C. O'Neil-Hart. 2017. "Marketing to Millennial Parents? Here's How They're Redefining Parenting for Their Generation." www .thinkwithgoogle.com/consumer-insights/marketing -millennial-parents-youtube-insights.

Halgunseth, L.C., A. Peterson, D.R. Stark, & S. Moodie. 2009. "Family Engagement, Diverse Families, and Early Childhood Education Programs: An Integrated Review of the Literature." Washington, DC: NAEYC & Pre-K Now.

Knowles, M.S., E.F. Holton III, & R.A. Swanson. 2005. *The Adult Learner: The Definitive Classic in Adult Education and Human Resource Development*. 6th ed. Waltham, MA: Butterworth-Heinemann.

Lally, J.R., & P.L. Mangione. 2017. "Caring Relationships: The Heart of Early Brain Development. *Young Children* 72 (2): 17–24.

Lally, J.R., J. Stewart, & D. Greenwald, eds. 2009. *Infant/Toddler Caregiving: A Guide to Setting Up Environments*. 2nd ed. Sacramento: California Department of Education.

Lopez, M.E., M. Caspe, & L. McWilliams. 2016. *Public Libraries: A Vital Space for Family Engagement*. Report. Cambridge, MA: Harvard Family Research Project. www.ala.org/pla/sites/ala.org.pla/files /content/initiatives/familyengagement/Public -Libraries-A-Vital-Space-for-Family-Engagement _HFRP-PLA_August-2-2016.pdf.

McKnight, K., N. Venkateswaran, J. Laird, J. Robles, & T. Shalev. 2017. *Mindset Shifts and Parent Teacher Home Visits,* Report. Research Triangle Park, NC: RTI International. www.pthvp.org/wp-content/uploads/2018 /02/PTHV_Study1_Report.pdf.

NAEYC. 2016. *Code of Ethical Conduct and Statement of Commitment.* Brochure. Rev. ed. Washington, DC: NAEYC.

NAEYC. 2018. "NAEYC Early Learning Program Accreditation Standards and Assessment Items." Washington, DC: NAEYC. www.naeyc.org/sites/default/files /globally-shared/downloads/PDFs/accreditation/early -learningstandards_and_assessment_web_1.pdf

NAEYC. n.d. "Principles of Effective Family Engagement." Washington, DC: NAEYC. NAEYC.org/resources/topics /family-engagement/principles.

NAEYC. 2009a. "Developmentally Appropriate Practice in Early Childhood Programs Serving Children from Birth through Age 8." Washington, DC: NAEYC.

NEA (National Education Association). n.d. "Research Spotlight on Home Visits." www.nea.org/tools/16935.htm.

Nemeth, K.N. 2016. "Top Tips for Translating Materials for Preschool DLLs and Families." *Language Castle* (blog). www.languagecastle.com/2016/09/top-tips-translating -materials-multilingual-preschool.

Nemeth, K.N. 2017. "Considering Children Who Are DLLs in Emergency Planning." *Language Castle* (blog). www .languagecastle.com/2017/09/considering-children-dlls -emergency-planning-2.

Nemeth, K.N. 2018. "Fast 5 Gamechangers that REALLY Get Parents of DLLs to Engage." Blog post. www.languagecastle .com/2014/09/fast-5-gamechangers-really-get-parents -dlls-engage.

Nemeth, K.N., & C. Campbell. 2013. "Get to Know the NEW Children's Librarian." *Teaching Young Children* 7 (2): 28.

Nimmo, J., & B. Hallett. 2008. "Childhood in the Garden: A Place to Encounter Natural and Social Diversity." *Young Children* 63 (1): 32–38.

Park, M., A. O'Toole, & C. Katsiaficas. 2017. *Dual Language Learners: A National Demographic and Policy Profile.* Fact sheet. Washington, DC: Migration Policy Institute. www .migrationpolicy.org/research/dual-language-learners -national-demographic-and-policy-profile.

PITC (Program for Infant/Toddler Care). n.d. "PITC's Six Program Policies." www.pitc.org/pub/pitc_docs/policies .html.

Saunders, J. 2017. "March DaDness: Engaging Fathers." *Teaching Young Children* 10 (3): 29–30.

Seplocha, H. 2004. "Partnerships for Learning: Conferencing with Families." *Young Children* 59 (5): 96–99.

US Department of Health and Human Services (DHHS), Administration for Children and Families (ACF), Children's Bureau. n.d. "Family Engagement Inventory." Washington, DC: DHHS, ACF, Children's Bureau. www.childwelfare.gov /fei/definition.

US Department of Health and Human Services (DHHS) & US Department of Education (DOE). 2016. "Policy Statement on Expulsion and Suspension Policies in Early Childhood Settings." Washington, DC: DHHS & DOE. www2.ed.gov /policy/gen/guid/school-discipline/policy-statement-ece -expulsions-suspensions.pdf.

US Department of Health and Human Services (DHHS) & US Department of Education (DOE). 2017. "Policy Statement on Supporting the Development of Children Who Are Dual Language Learners in Early Childhood Programs." Policy statement. Washington, DC: DHHS & DOE. www.acf.hhs .gov/sites/default/files/ecd/dll_policy_statement_final.pdf.

US Office of Head Start (OHS). 2016. *Head Start Program Performance Standards.* Washington, DC: OHS. http://eclkc.ohs.acf.hhs.gov/policy/45-cfr-chap-xiii.

Valente, J.M. 2018. "Mr. Joe Becomes a Dad: A Former Preschool Teacher Reflects on His First Child Starting School." *Young Children* 73 (4): 6–11.

Van Voorhis, F.L., M.F. Maier, J.L. Epstein, & C.M. Lloyd. 2013. *The Impact of Family Involvement on the Education of Children Ages 3 to 8: A Focus on Literacy and Math Achievement Outcomes and Social-Emotional Skills.* Report. New York: MDRC. http://dev.mdrc.org/sites /default/files/The_Impact_of_Family_Involvement _FR.pdf.

Washington, V., ed. 2017. *Essentials for Working with Young Childen.* 2nd ed. Washington, DC: The Council for Professional Recognition.

Weiss, H.B., M.E. Lopez, & H. Rosenberg. 2010. "Beyond Random Acts: Family, School, and Community Engagement as an Integral Part of Education Reform." Paper. Cambridge, MA: Harvard Family Research Project. www .sedl.org/connections/engagement_forum/beyond _random_acts.pdf.

Weyer, M. 2015. "Engaging Families in Education." Policy paper. Denver, CO: National Conference of State Legislators. www.ncsl.org/Portals/1/Documents/educ /Engaging_Families_Education.pdf.

ZERO TO THREE & Bezos Family Foundation. 2016. *Tuning In: Parents of Young Children Tell Us What They Think, Know, and Need.* Report. Washington, DC: ZERO TO THREE & Bezos Family Foundation. www.zerotothree.org /resources/series/tuning-in-parents-of-young-children -tell-us-what-they-think-know-and-need.

Acknowledgments

We would like to thank the many early childhood professionals and programs with whom we have engaged throughout our careers, especially Sunbeam Family Services Early Childhood Program and Oklahoma City Educare, whose insights guided our writing. We are grateful for the accounts of family engagement practices from Valeria Erdosi-Mehaffey of The King's Daughters Day School; Kara Ahmed of the NYC Department of Education's LYFE program; Rosanne Hansel about a story from the Universal Studios Child Care Center; and the staff of the Phillipsburg Early Childhood Program at the Early Childhood Learning Center in Phillipsburg, NJ.

In addition, we greatly appreciate the contributions of the early childhood professionals who provided contacts with educators who could provide examples of how they addressed challenges in engaging families. Peg Callaghan, Jerlean Daniel, Judy Davis, Jan Greenberg, Whit Hayslip, Judy Jablon, Colleen Young, and Aisha White helped us reach out to the following early childhood educators who eagerly shared their experiences:

> Ana Azcarate, President Avenue Elementary School, Harbor City, CA

> Shannon C.M. Banks, ReadySteps Program, ReadyKids, Inc., Charlottesville, VA

> Dawn Brown, Christ the King Early Education Center, Topeka, KS

> Tracy Ehlert, B2K Learning Center, Cedar Rapids, IA

> Samantha Ellwood, Providence Connections, Pittsburgh, PA

> Renate Engels, Guadalupe Center, Immokalee, FL

> Stephanie Geneseo, All Nestled Inn Family Child Care, Chesapeake, OH

> Linda Gillespie, Family and Infant Development Specialist, West Stockbridge, MA

> Jamie Hartley, Methodist Day School, Portland, TX Jamie Hartley is the director of the Methodist Day School (MDS) in

> Valerie Rocio Harvey, Expanded Transitional Kindergarten/Preschool Class, Lankershim Elementary School, North Hollywood CA

> Donna King, Children First, Durham, NC

> Jenny Levinson, Wintonbury Early Childhood Magnet School, Bloomfield, CT

> Julia Luckenbill, The Center for Child and Family Studies, University of California, Davis

> Lynn A. Manfredi/Petitt, The Creative Comfy Day School @ Lynn's House, Decatur, GA

> Melissa Russell, The Hundred Acre School at Heritage Museums and Gardens, Sandwich, MA

> Debbie Walsh, Green Acres School, Rockville, MD

> Monica Warren, Crisp County Pre-K, Cordele, GA

> Dee Dee Parker Wright, Jubilee JumpStart, Washington, DC

Lastly, we extend our sincere gratitude to Kathy Charner and her colleagues at NAEYC, who sustained the vision for this book. They helped us take the content from a spark of an idea through all the writing and editing stages that resulted in publication of this book. And, they helped us keep goals, audiences, and language in mind as we shared our ideas and those from early childhood educators who work with children and engage families.

About the Authors

Derry Koralek is president of DGK & Company, providing early childhood educational consulting to a variety of clients, including teachers and family child care providers. She is author of a number of early childhood resources, including two books cowritten with Laura J. Colker, *High-Quality Early Childhood Programs: The What, Why, and How* (2018), and *Making Lemonade: Teaching Young Children to Think Optimistically* (2019). Her other recent work includes developing training materials for staff in Early Head Start and revising the textbook, *Essentials for Working with Young Children*. For 14 years, Derry wrote, edited, and managed publications for the National Association for the Education of Young Children (NAEYC). She joined NAEYC as editor in chief of *Young Children*, the association's award-winning, peer-reviewed professional journal, and later also created and served as editor in chief of *Teaching Young Children*, NAEYC's magazine for preschool educators. During her time at NAEYC, Derry also became chief publishing officer, directing all print and digital publications. Before joining NAEYC, Koralek completed numerous projects through DGK & Company in support of early childhood teachers and family child care providers.

Karen Nemeth, EdM, is an author and speaker with a passion for supporting young children from diverse linguistic and cultural backgrounds in early childhood education. She has spent decades working with organizations, schools, Head Start programs, and government agencies across the United States and beyond to improve policies and practices that support children and their families. Her consultation with urban, rural, and suburban programs has given her valuable insights about the role of families in their child's early education and the role of teachers in welcoming and engaging those families. Karen has held leadership roles in NAEYC, the National Association for Bilingual Education (NABE), TESOL International Association, and several state organizations. She has written more than ten books and many articles in support of the field. Previously, she has worked for the National Center on Early Childhood Development, Teaching, and Learning; the New Jersey Department of Education; Community Coordinated Child Care of Union County; North Jersey Community Coordinated Child Care; and Felician University. Her greatest joy is the time she spends building spaceships and exploring nature with her five grandchildren.

Kelly Ramsey began her work with children and families as an early childhood teacher in 1984. For more than 20 years, she has had the opportunity to work with children and families as a classroom teacher, center director, family educator, mentor coach, and college instructor. As a lifelong learner, Kelly believes that self-discovery and personal reflection are key to creating rich learning environments for adults and children. She has a strong interest in families and their strength in nurturing children's development. As a passionate teacher, focused visionary, and a purpose-driven leader, she fosters engaging learning environments that help individuals to grow. As a family educator, she believes in engaging families and educators to develop intentional interactions between school and home. Kelly is a storyteller who shares her experiences as a preschool teacher, center director, and mother of two amazing young children. She fosters a welcoming environment for all types of learners, embracing the experiences of each individual and challenging learners by creating rich experiences and dialogues that connect theory to practice.

NAEYC's Bestselling Books

Great Books for Preschool and Kindergarten Teachers

Item 1132 • 2017 • 160 pages

Big Questions for Young Minds

Questions are powerful tools, especially in the classroom. Asking rich, thoughtful questions can spark young children's natural curiosity and illuminate a whole new world of possibility and insight. But what are "big" questions, and how do they encourage children to think deeply? With this intentional approach—rooted in Bloom's Taxonomy—teachers working with children ages 3 through 6 will discover how to meet children at their individual developmental levels and stretch their thinking. With the guidance in this book as a cornerstone in your day-to-day teaching practices, learn how to be more intentional in your teaching, scaffold children's learning, and promote deeper understanding.

Finally, a resource to help teachers develop and ask questions that encourage children to think, imagine, and generate ideas!
—Beth G.

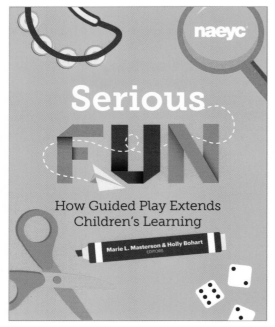

Item 1137 • 2019 • 144 pages

Serious Fun

What emerges when we combine child choice in play with teachers' intentional guidance? Guided play—a powerful tool to help children learn essential knowledge and skills in the context of playful situations.

This book illustrates strategies for providing content-rich, joyful learning experiences, such as setting up play environments with learning goals in mind and offering suggestions and questions during play to prompt deeper learning. It also offers ways to share with families the importance of play for all areas of learning. There are many ways for children to play—dive into the exciting possibilities of guided play.

. . . Demonstrates the importance not only of play but also of teachers' roles as intentional facilitators. —Noelle W.

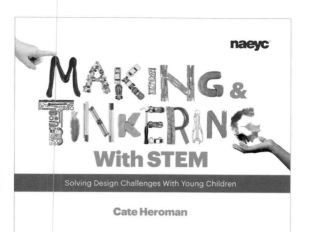

Item 1130 • 2017 • 144 pages

Making & Tinkering With STEM

Explore science, technology, engineering, and math (STEM) concepts through making and tinkering! With 25 classroom-ready engineering design challenges inspired by children's favorite books, educators can seamlessly integrate making and tinkering and STEM concepts in preschool through third grade classrooms. Challenge children to use everyday materials and STEM concepts to design and build solutions to problems faced by characters in their favorite books. This practical, hands-on resource includes

› 25 engineering design challenges appropriate for children ages 3–8
› Suggestions for creating a makerspace environment for children
› A list of 100 picture books that encourage STEM-rich exploration and learning
› Questions and ideas for expanding children's understanding of STEM concepts

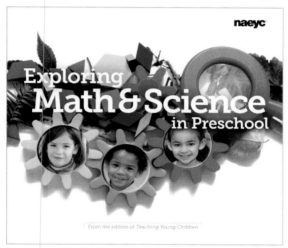

Item 7226 • 2015 • 112 pages

Exploring Math & Science in Preschool

What every preschool teacher needs! Filled with practical strategies and useful information on math and science, including

› Learning center ideas
› Engaging activities
› Ideas that support the development and learning of every preschooler
› Children's book recommendations

This excellent resource of engaging math and science learning experiences for preschoolers was developed for you by the editors of *Teaching Young Children*.

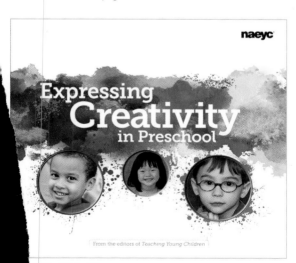

7225 • 2015 • 128 pages

Expressing Creativity in Preschool

What every preschool teacher needs! Filled with practical strategies and useful information on art, music and movement, and dramatic play, this book offers

› Learning center ideas
› Engaging activities
› Practical suggestions that are easy to implement
› Ideas that support the development and learning of every preschooler
› Children's book recommendations

This excellent resource of engaging learning experiences for preschoolers was developed for you by the editors of *Teaching Young Children*.

Discover NAEYC!

The National Association for the Education of Young Children (NAEYC) promotes high-quality early learning for all young children, birth through age 8, by connecting early childhood practice, policy, and research. We advance a diverse, dynamic early childhood profession and support all who care for, educate, and work on behalf of young children.

NAEYC members have access to award-winning publications, professional development, networking opportunities, professional liability insurance, and an array of members-only discounts.

Accreditation—NAEYC.org/accreditation

Across the country, **NAEYC Accreditation of Early Learning Programs** and **NAEYC Accreditation of Early Childhood Higher Education Programs** set the industry standards for quality in early childhood education. These systems use research-based standards to recognize excellence in the field of early childhood education.

Advocacy and Public Policy—NAEYC.org/policy

NAEYC is a leader in promoting and advocating for policies at the local, state, and federal levels that expand opportunities for all children to have equitable access to high-quality early learning. NAEYC is also dedicated to promoting policies that value early childhood educators and support their excellence.

Global Engagement—NAEYC.org/global

NAEYC's Global Engagement department works with governments and other large-scale systems to create guidelines to support early learning, as well as early childhood professionals throughout the world.

Professional Learning—NAEYC.org/ecp

NAEYC provides face-to-face training, technology-based learning, and Accreditation workshops—all leading to improvements in the knowledge, skills, and practices of early childhood professionals.

Publications and Resources—NAEYC.org/publications

NAEYC publishes some of the most valued resources for early childhood professionals, including award-winning books, *Teaching Young Children* magazine, and *Young Children*, the association's peer-reviewed journal. NAEYC publications focus on developmentally appropriate practice and enable members to stay up to date on current research and emerging trends, with information they can apply directly to their classroom practice.

Signature Events—NAEYC.org/events

NAEYC hosts three of the most important and well-attended annual events for educators, students, administrators, and advocates in the early learning community.

NAEYC's Annual Conference is the world's largest gathering of early childhood professionals.

NAEYC's Professional Learning Institute is the premier professional development conference for early childhood trainers, faculty members, researchers, systems administrators, and other professionals.

The **NAEYC Public Policy Forum** provides members with resources, training, and networking opportunities to build advocacy skills and relationships with policymakers on Capitol Hill.

Membership Options/Benefits

NAEYC.org/membership

NAEYC offers four membership categories*—Entry Level, Standard, Premium, and Family—each with a unique set of benefits.

	ENTRY $30	STANDARD $69	PREMIUM $150	FAMILY $35
Digital Articles of *YC* & *TYC*	●	●	●	●
Online Networking	●	●	●	●
Local Affiliate Membership	●	●	●	●
Naeyc Store Discounts	●	●	●	●
Discount Insurance & Subscriptions	●	●	●	●
Retail Discounts	●	●	●	●
Naeyc Event Discounts	○	●	●	○
Complimentary Naeyc Books	○	◐ 1 book	● 5 books	○
Print Subscription to *YC* or *TYC*	○	◐ Either	● Both	○
Online Courses	○	◐ 1 course	● 2 courses	○
Access to *YC* Digital Archive	○	●	●	○
Access to VIP Events	○	○	●	○

*Prices and benefits are subject to change. Check NAEYC.org for the most current information.